Growing

INTO HIS

Likeness

ISBN: 978-1-949648-97-3

Cover and text layout design: Kristi Yoder

Printed in the USA

Published by:
TGS International
P.O. Box 355
Berlin, Ohio 44610 USA
Phone: 330.893.4828
Fax: 330.893.2305
www.tgsinternational.com

TGS002024

WILMA WEBB

Growing INTO HIS Likeness

Devotional thoughts for women

Acknowledgments

A special thanks to CAM-TGS International for printing this book, and to the reviewers and editors who worked with me so graciously to improve it.

I thank my husband, Lloyd, for all his encouragement, and grandson Zac for coming so often to offer his computer expertise. I couldn't have done it without you, Zac.

To the Lord Jesus Christ, I offer all praise, honor, and glory for it was He who led me as I studied His precious Word. I pray this book can be a blessing to all who read it.

—a sister in Christ,
Wilma Webb

Introduction

It is ever the heart cry of our heavenly Father for us to come closer to Him. James 4:8 promises that if we will draw near to God, He will draw near to us. If we feel coolness in our relationship with God, it is not because He has moved, but we have stepped away. I pray that the words of this book will help you to step closer to the Savior's side and to grow into His likeness.

Growing is not always an easy process. Sometimes it is painful, but, oh, it's worth the struggle! As we honor God with our obedience and devoted love, we are blessed beyond measure as His beloved daughters. Allow the things that hinder you to fall aside, and press ever closer to the heart of God. Keep growing, dear sisters!

—a sister in Christ,
Wilma Webb

Table of Contents

1. The Invitation 14
2. Sin in Paradise...16
3. Consequences of Sin 18
4. The Only Way Back 20
5. Just One Taste...22
6. Experiencing Christ's Love 24
7. Accept My Yoke...26
8. A Love Letter 28
9. Listening to God..30
10. True Worship 32
11. The Love of Money 34
12. My Money or God's?..36
13. Worship God Through Giving...............................38
14. Praise or Pout?..40
15. Sing Unto the Lord 42
16. Phone Line to God...44
17. Choices and Outcomes 46
18. Blockage in the Line...48
19. A Broken and a Contrite Heart 50
20. Under the Knife...52
21. God's Chastening Hand.......................................54
22. Death and Grief—Our Teachers...........................56

23.	Abiding in the Vine	58
24.	Puzzle Pieces	60
25.	A Lacy Snare	62
26.	An Insatiable Appetite	64
27.	Truth We Can Rely On	66
28.	One Body, One Lord	68
29.	Who Has Your Heart?	70
30.	Staying Within God's Parameters	72
31.	The Righteous in This Generation	74
32.	Rewards of the Righteous	76
33.	Where Is Your Name Written?	78
34.	Through Afflictions	80
35.	Salvation and Song	82
36.	Grace and Truth	84
37.	Unfailing Faithfulness	86
38.	The Temple of the Lord	88
39.	Exalt the Lord	90
40.	Confessing Our Faults	92
41.	Bringing Hope	94
42.	God's People	96
43.	Bow Down Your Ear	98
44.	God's Sheltering Wings	100
45.	Beautiful Hands	102
46.	Our God Is So Big	104
47.	Deep Cleaning	106
48.	The Cost of Obedience	108
49.	Instrument of Torture	110
50.	Denying Self	112
51.	Jars of Clay	114
52.	Counted Worthy	116
53.	This Moment of Time	118
54.	"I Am Persuaded"	120
55.	Procrastination	122
56.	Watch and Pray	124

57.	At Midnight	126
58.	Nothing Between	128
59.	God's Plan for You	130
60.	A Virtuous Woman	132
61.	Evidence of Transformation	134
62.	What Family Do You Resemble?	136
63.	Reality of Marriage	138
64.	The Sanctity of Marriage	140
65.	Love That Endures	142
66.	Finding Our All in Christ	144
67.	Maintaining Moral Purity	146
68.	Impelling Love	148
69.	A Wise Woman	150
70.	Beams of Light	152
71.	Walk Circumspectly	154
72.	A Beautiful Bride	156
73.	God's Plan Is Best	158
74.	Returning Christ's Love	160
75.	A Sure Foundation	162
76.	Pink Walls and Appreciation	164
77.	Hanging Pictures	166
78.	The Flopped Pie	168
79.	In the Doghouse	170
80.	How's the Atmosphere?	172
81.	Tornado Watch	174
82.	The Love of Family	176
83.	Loving Our Children	178
84.	Ideals for Our Children	180
85.	Danger! Poison!	182
86.	Precious in His Sight	184
87.	Lord, Be Merciful	186
88.	The Place to Find Wisdom	188
89.	A Pure Heart	190
90.	Road Closed Ahead	192

91.	True Happiness	194
92.	What Are You Wearing?	196
93.	Behind the Door	198
94.	Garage Sale Today	200
95.	If You Want Greatness	202
96.	Learning from Life's Experiences	204
97.	Blooming Where God Places You	206
98.	In His Garden	208
99.	A Pattern of Good Works	210
100.	The Grace of Patience	212
101.	Who Is Watching You?	214
102.	Faith That Heals	216
103.	True Friendship	218
104.	Judging and Grudging	220
105.	Living in Peace	222
106.	Instruments for God's Glory	224
107.	Waiting on the Lord	226
108.	Contentment	228
109.	Bigger and Better	230
110.	Showing Hospitality	232
111.	The Joy of Giving	234
112.	God's Eye Is on the Widow	236
113.	An Evening Song	238
114.	Christ, Our Anchor	240
115.	What Is Your Score?	242
116.	The Angels Rejoice	244
117.	A Holy Calling	246
118.	Bound by Sin	248
119.	Till the Dawn	250
	Index to Scripture Readings	253
	Endnotes	255
	About the Author	257

The Invitation

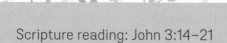

The large, cream-colored envelope in the mailbox attracted my attention. Thick paper, a special stamp, the sticker with intertwined hearts—all whispered, "Someone wants you to share in something special." I slit the envelope flap and the invitation slid into my eager hands. I was honored to be among those invited to my friends' wedding.

Invitations we receive for earthly events can be accepted—or ignored. However, there is one invitation we dare not ignore, for life or death depends on it. God invites "whosoever will" to come to Him through His Son. Because our great Creator loves us so very much, He sent His only Son to earth to teach us, love us, and show us the way to God. He calls us to respond to that love.

Christ Jesus, the Son of God, willingly died on the cross to free us from our sin. He rose from the grave to let us know He has conquered sin and death. Today He sits by His Father God, desiring for each of us to believe in Him.

John the Baptist told the crowd at the Jordan River, "He that believeth on the Son hath everlasting life: and he that believeth not the Son shall not see life; but the wrath of God abideth on him" (John 3:36).

God offers us everlasting life through His Son. The invitation has been given to all. But because God is just, He cannot overlook sin. He freely offers forgiveness and cleansing if we come to Him in repentance.

We have everything to gain when we accept His invitation, and everything to lose if we refuse. We can never gain heaven by our own merits. We are helpless to save ourselves. We need a Savior.

What will you do with God's invitation? Remember, your response determines your destiny. Today is the day to respond, for you have no promise of tomorrow. God is eagerly waiting for you to accept His invitation.

One day Christ will return for His bride, the church made up of all those who have accepted the invitation. Will you be present at the most glorious banquet of all—the wedding supper of the Lamb? You don't want to miss it!

Dear heavenly Father, I accept your invitation. I believe in you. I want to be part of your bride, the church, and have life everlasting. I want to be ready for your return. Thank you for dying for me so I can come to you. In Jesus' name, Amen.

Because of love, our Father God
Sent Christ His Son to earth
To break the power of sin and death,
To offer us new birth.

Sin in Paradise

*R*ita softly closed her bedroom door, furtively glancing out the window. *Good! Mom is in the garden.* Opening a dresser drawer, she reached under a stack of sweaters and drew out a small book. *Now, if I can just have a few minutes, I can finish this chapter. I wonder if Sue is going to sneak out to meet Sam.*

"Rita, where are you?" Her mother's voice floated up the stairs. "Could you come and help us snap beans, please?"

"Oh, no!" Rita groaned. "There's never time to read." Sighing, she called, "Coming, Mom." Slipping the book back into its hiding place, her conscience pricked. *Mom and Dad would not approve of this book.* But another voice argued, *It's not that bad. I want to read it. It's so thrilling!*

Before Rita had been lured into reading novels, she had sung hymns as she worked and enjoyed spending time in prayer. But now she allowed herself to fantasize, wishing she could live the life of the girl in her latest book. Rita, like Eve, was listening to Satan, considering his words, and eating forbidden fruit.

Long ago in the Garden of Eden, Eve shared the forbidden fruit with Adam—and they both shared the terrible consequences. Adam too, was guilty; he knew better than Eve that he was doing wrong. The awful weight of guilt and fear settled in their trembling hearts. They dreaded the evening, when God would come to the garden to walk and talk with them. And so they tried to hide, tried to cover their shame. Their connection with God had been severed. But God knew exactly where they were and what they had done, and He sought them and called to them.

God seeks and calls us today. When sin opens a chasm between us and God, we sometimes put on a front. We can regularly attend church, we can even mouth a daily prayer—but if we tolerate sin in our lives, we court destruction. Like Rita, we may try to hide our sin, but our Father knows everything about us. We cannot hide anything from Him.

Has sin separated you from God? Are you struggling with temptation? Only Christ can set you free, and He longs to hear your plea for forgiveness. He wants to bring you back into closeness with the Father. Won't you cry out to God today and find His sweet peace again?

Dear heavenly Father, please forgive me. I have allowed things in my life to draw me away from you. I know they are wrong, and I confess them as sin. I need you, Jesus. I am helpless without you. Please restore my fellowship with you. In Jesus' name, Amen.

We must each day be on our guard,
    And near the Savior stay;
He'll give us strength to overcome
    And keep us lest we stray.

Consequences of Sin

The massive walls of Jericho had crumbled! Joshua 6 gives the story of this amazing event. The people of Israel had marched around the city every day for a week, and on the seventh day they had compassed it seven times. When they shouted, down came the walls, and Israelite men swarmed into the city. God had given them a miraculous victory!

Soon after the triumph at Jericho, Joshua sent a small army of three thousand to fight the tiny city of Ai (Joshua 7). They should have easily conquered the city. Instead, the men of the city chased them, killing some and terrorizing others.

What went wrong? Why had God allowed this? Joshua tore his clothes and fell with his face to the ground, devastated that his men had turned their backs and run from the battle. But God told him in essence, "Get up! Sin is in the camp—and you need to deal with it" (Joshua 7:10–13). God would not bless Israel with victory while sin remained hidden.

Joshua discovered that a man from the tribe of Judah had coveted some forbidden spoils at Jericho. Achan had taken them and hidden them beneath his tent, but they were not hidden from God's eyes. Achan's disobedience affected him, his family, and the whole army of Israel. God ordered that Achan and his family be stoned; all his belongings and the stolen objects, burned. A great pile of stones heaped upon the spot reminded Israel of the cost of one man's sin.

When we are tempted to excuse wrongdoing with the thought, "What I'm doing isn't hurting anyone else," we should remember Achan. We may try to justify what we do, downplay the seriousness of it, or try to convince ourselves it will be all right, but God sees through our excuses. Hidden sin blocks our fellowship with God and with other believers. "If we say we have fellowship with him, and walk in darkness, we lie, and do not the truth" (1 John 1:6).

Are you harboring sin in your life? Is anything hindering you from free and open communion with God? "God is faithful and just to forgive us our sins, and to cleanse us from all unrighteousness" (1 John 1:9). God desires your wholehearted devotion. Christ is waiting to forgive.

> *Dear Lord, I am sorry for my disobedience to your Word.*
> *Please forgive me, and give me victory over sin. Thank*
> *you for your love and mercy to me.*
> *In Christ's name, Amen.*

Our God desires obedience;
   He wants our hearts to be
Committed wholly unto Him;
   This will our Father please.
Into our very minds and souls
   The heavenly Father sees.
If we have sinned, we must repent
   And fall on bended knees.

The Only Way Back

King David knew all along that he was toying with sin. From the moment he lusted after Bathsheba until he planned the murder of her husband Uriah, he knew he was doing wrong. Perhaps he tried to quell his conscience by listening to the tempter's excuses. *Look, you're the king. You have the right to any woman you want. So what if she has a husband? Just put him into the heat of the battle. When he is killed, your problem is solved.*

An allegory by the faithful prophet Nathan opened David's eyes to the gravity of his sins. Then he cried, "I have sinned against the LORD" (2 Samuel 12:13). David pled with God to wash him thoroughly from iniquity and cleanse him from his sin: "For I acknowledge my transgressions: and my sin is ever before me" (Psalm 51:3). David no longer made excuses for his sin.

Have you, like David, lost your way and found yourself out of touch with God? Only true repentance will open the way back. This means recognizing and sorrowing over your wrong thoughts or actions, and desiring to change your ways.

David asked God to restore the joy of his salvation (Psalm 51:12). He realized he had lost his closeness and joy in God. If we are honest with ourselves when we have sinned, we will sense our loss of joy and delight in God. The Word becomes stale, and our prayer time falters. Church attendance becomes a duty rather than a delight.

God accepts nothing—money, time, or good deeds—in place of repentance. We cannot cover our sin by doing things for God. He wants our brokenness. "The sacrifices of God are a broken spirit: a broken and a contrite heart, O God, thou wilt not despise" (Psalm 51:17).

Are you experiencing the joy and peace of God? Are you delighting yourself in the Lord? If not, won't you come back to God? Humble yourself, and seek His forgiveness. He is waiting for you with open arms.

Dear Lord, please forgive my sins. Cleanse me, and restore to me the joy of fellowship with you. I want to draw closer to you today. In Jesus' name, Amen.

Just as I am! without one plea,
But that Thy blood was shed for me,
And that thou bidd'st me come to Thee,
O Lamb of God, I come! I come!

Just as I am! Thy love unknown
Has broken every barrier down;
Now to be Thine, yea, Thine alone,
O Lamb of God, I come! I come![a]

—Charlotte Elliott

[a] All song lyrics used in this book are from public domain, unless otherwise noted.

Just One Taste

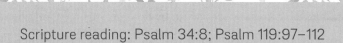

I opened my sister's refrigerator and discovered a lime jello salad sitting on the top shelf. I tested a tiny spoonful. Mmm! It tasted as delicious as it looked.

I was babysitting my three nieces that day. But when I set that delectable salad on the table, my oldest niece shuddered. "I don't want any of that green stuff, thank you," she announced. I tried to get her to take just one bite, but she refused. Not one spoonful of it would pass her lips. Today we laugh about this episode, but she still doesn't like lime jello.

While caring for my grandchildren, I sometimes try to interest them in a new food. If they take just a small bite, they usually respond, "That's pretty good. I'll take some more, please."

Sometimes people are hesitant to "taste" God's Word. They may consider it old-fashioned, behind the times, hard to digest, or just a book of fables. However, those who taste God's Word and experience its truth say with the writer of Psalm 119:103, "How sweet are thy words unto my taste! Yea, sweeter than honey to my mouth!" Those who nourish themselves with Scripture find their appetites whetted for more.

The Word of God satisfies our souls and gives us spiritual nutrition to survive and grow. It adds vitality to our lives. Psalm 119:97 says, "O how love I thy law! It is my meditation all the day." (As I was typing this verse, I accidentally wrote "medication." God's Word is that too!) "This is my comfort in my affliction: for thy word hath quickened me" (Psalm 119:50). The word *quickened* means to give life.

Feasting on God's Word provides life and strength for the day, light for the way, and hope for the future. (See Psalm 119:5.) "Thy word is very pure: therefore thy servant loveth it" (Psalm 119:140). Richer nutrition does not exist!

Your diet affects you negatively or positively. What are you feeding upon? Taste and savor God's Word. You will find it's what you need to guide your steps aright.

> *Dear Lord, thank you for your wonderful words of life. One taste makes me crave more! Help me to feed on it regularly. In Jesus' name, Amen.*

We have the Bible, God's own Word,
　　To teach us right from wrong,
To tell us of the Savior's love,
　　To cheer, and make us strong.

23

Experiencing Christ's Love

"Jesus is offering you forgiveness, healing, hope. Will you surrender your all to Him?" The minister's earnest words at the close of his message seemed to single me out. From childhood I had sung and believed the familiar words, "Jesus loves me, this I know," but that evening I understood for the first time how desperately I needed a Savior. But questions still troubled me. What would my teenage peers say? Could I remain faithful to Christ?

Yet I could not ignore the yearning in my soul. How I wanted to publicly declare my decision to follow Jesus! I knew only Christ's blood could wash away my sin. That night I yielded to Christ's call. I felt God's love, experienced His pardon, and found a joy I never knew existed. I truly became a new creation!

In the public school cafeteria the following day, I told my friends what had happened to me. I wanted the whole world to know what Jesus had done for me and what He could do for them.

"Well, I belong to a church, so I'm fine," one of them shrugged. Another claimed she didn't need to go to church. A few thought it was fine for me, but they didn't want to be so radical. "My life doesn't need to change just because I believe Jesus is the Son of God," one friend told me.

I left the conversation heavy-hearted. How could they reject such life-changing love? How could they slap their Savior in the face with their nonchalance and disinterest? I knew I had something real. Christ's love had transformed my heart, giving me new desires. I didn't want my old life. Instead, I wanted to love and please my Lord forever.

Fifty-seven years have passed since I found Christ as my Savior. How precious He is to me! He is my dearest Friend. His love has never failed me in all these years.

Love between us and God flows both ways. If we love Him and keep His commandments, Christ will dwell with us (John 14:23).

Do you still marvel at His potent love, displayed on Calvary? Do you praise Him for that love every day? Is your relationship with Him blooming? Is your service motivated by heartfelt devotion, or by a mere sense of duty? He loved you first—how can you not love Him and yield to Him your all?

Dear Lord, thank you for forgiving my sins and giving me joy. Help me to be faithful, abiding with you. In Jesus' name, Amen.

The love of God—it is too great
    For minds to comprehend;
Yet God desires to make His home
    Within the hearts of men.

Accept My Yoke

*P*icture two oxen—one mature, the other young and untried— being yoked together and hitched to a heavily-loaded wagon. The young ox bellows his displeasure, twisting and turning in an effort to shake off the yoke. He wants to kick up his heels and run.

The older ox meekly accepts the yoke. His eyes follow his master's movements with subdued trust. At his master's command, he begins to pull the heavy load in spite of his partner's skittishness. Finally, accepting his fate, the young ox tries to match his elder's pace. He leans into the yoke. To his surprise, it is easier than he thought.

Jesus says, "Take my yoke upon you, and learn of me; for I am meek and lowly in heart: and ye shall find rest unto your souls. For my yoke is easy, and my burden is light" (Matthew 11:29–30).

Will we submit to His yoke and follow Him in meekness and humility? Christ longs to give us rest, but the choice is ours. When we chafe at the circumstances He ordains and harden our necks to His direction, we only make ourselves miserable. When we cling to our pride and stubbornness, we encounter God's resistance (James 4:6). If we accept His yoke and depend upon His strength, our burdens become lighter. Christ gives us His yoke in love and mercy. Obeying His commandments, we thrive.

Philippians 2:5–8 outlines how Christ lived out humility. He left the splendor of heaven to become a servant of men, laying down His life for our sins. Although men criticized, threatened, and abused Him, Christ submitted to their treatment. He prayed on the cross for God to forgive those who crucified Him. His example compels us to submit and forgive.

At the end of day, oxen are led to the barn for food, water, and rest. We, too, are offered rest—now and in the future. Christ gives us rest in our souls when we come to Him. No longer need we carry the torturous burdens of guilt, fear, and bitterness. Not only does Christ offer us deliverance and freedom, but He also promises eternal rest in the home He has prepared for those who believe in Him. Today He calls, "Come unto me . . . and I will give you rest. Take my yoke upon you, and learn of me" (Matthew 11:28–29).

Do you find it hard to kick against the goads? Are you ready to be delivered, as one author put it, from the "terrible burden of always needing to get [your] own way"?[1] Won't you accept Christ's yoke today?

Dear Lord, today I surrender my will to yours. I accept your yoke. Help me to learn by your example so I can live to glorify your name. In Christ's name, Amen.

Accept the yoke, dear one;
  Find succor, child oppressed.
Come and learn humility,
  Then enter into rest.

A Love Letter

An elegant envelope addressed in a manly scrawl, a lovely greeting card with a letter inside—what young lady's heart does not skip a beat as she unfolds a message from her lover? A courting couple reads each other's letters to discover the other's likes and dislikes, preferences and convictions. Together they share dreams for the future.

God has also sent us a love letter—His Word. God reveals Himself on its pages, drawing us into a friendship with Him, as the disciples did with Jesus. The disciples knew their Master intimately (1 John 1). They walked with Him throughout His ministry. They watched Him die, and saw Him after His resurrection. The intimacy they shared with Christ and His Father is accessible to each one of us. God desires us to draw closer to Him. When we do, our joy will be full.

God's purposes in writing us this letter go far beyond generating warm feelings. He expects us to obey and honor Him. His truth defends us; when we study and absorb His Word, it becomes a sword which we must wield against our enemy, Satan. King David learned this, for he wrote, "Thy word have I hid in mine heart, that I might not sin against thee" (Psalm 119:11). For a weapon to be effective, we must be very familiar with it so we can use it quickly, instinctively. That requires time and meditation.

In this fast-changing world, what a comfort to know God's Word will never change! (See Psalm 119:89.) The truth we find there remains timeless—apt direction for us today. Psalm 119:105 says, "Thy word is a lamp unto my feet, and a light unto my path." God desires us to search His Word for gems of truth and comforting balm for our pain. Read and ponder His letter of love to you, and you'll find yourself drawn closer to the heart of God.

Dear Lord, thank you for your Word. Help me to study it more diligently and grow closer to you. In Jesus' name, Amen.

Your Word is Life to us, O Lord,
    The Bread on which we feed;
It nourishes our very soul,
    And meets our every need.

Listening to God

The child tugged on his mother's skirt. "Mommy, listen!" His mother, engrossed in conversation with a friend, remained oblivious to his need. How wonderful to know God listens when we cry out to Him!

Now, what about our side of the relationship? Do we listen to God, or are we too busy, too caught up with gardening, childcare, or social media? What does it take for God to get our attention?

God told the erring Israelites, "Hearken unto me" (Isaiah 46:3). In our day we would say, "Listen to me!" Only those who pay attention and obey can experience God's blessing. In Isaiah's day the Israelites knew they were hearing Jehovah's direct words through His prophets, yet they still went their own way.

Today we hear God's voice through different means. Perhaps we hear a moving sermon, but in a day or two we forget what touched us. Or we read an inspiring book and think, "I want to be like that," but we return to the same old ruts. Maybe we feel a stirring in our hearts when we read something in the Bible, and we are determined to improve in that area. But we go about our day and allow other pursuits to distract us from the conviction we felt. When God speaks to us, do we take it to heart and live it out?

Jesus compared one who ignores and disobeys God's commands with a man who chooses sand for the foundation of his house (Matthew

7:26). The foolish think, "I don't need to listen" (Proverbs 23:9).

In Psalm 143:8, David prays, "Cause me to hear thy lovingkindness in the morning; for in thee do I trust: cause me to know the way wherein I should walk; for I lift up my soul unto thee." David discovered the blessing of listening to God, and he found direction for his life. How seriously do we take God's Word?

How can we maintain a close relationship with the heavenly Father if we ignore His words? Jesus said, "He that rejecteth me, and receiveth not my words, hath one that judgeth him: the word that I have spoken, the same shall judge him in the last day" (John 12:48). We must take seriously every word of God. Are you listening?

> *Dear heavenly Father, help me to truly listen to you and*
> *obey with all my heart. In Jesus' name, Amen.*

Do we hear the Savior speaking
    In the quiet of the night?
Do we seek Him in the morning
    With desire and delight?

Through the day in all we're doing,
    Do we hear His quiet voice?
Do we yearn to know Him better?
    Will we make His way our choice?

If we'll heed the words He whispers,
    And His every charge obey,
We will find we're drawing closer;
    He'll abide with us for aye.

31

True Worship

The Jones family took their usual places in church, sang the familiar hymns, knelt to pray, and appeared attentive to the sermon. They worshiped God. Or . . . did they? Mr. Jones planned his work for the next day while his wife worried about the roast in the oven at home. Teenage daughter Jennie doodled in her notebook and wondered if anyone noticed her new dress. Son Dan checked out the visiting girls, hoping to be the first to talk to them after church.

After the service Mr. Jones went out of his way to avoid a fellow member against whom he held a grudge. Mrs. Jones felt slighted when the pastor's wife walked past her without a word and greeted a visitor instead. Jennie spoke sharply to the child who tugged at her skirt, worried he would wrinkle her dress. She ignored his hurt look. Dan felt annoyed and impatient with the elderly man who stopped to talk to him, delaying him from introducing himself to the new girls.

Did the Jones family truly worship that morning? Were their hearts touched?

God created us with an impulse to worship, but He gave us free will to choose the object of our worship. Too often we enthrone self instead of God. We pursue our own desires or wishes instead of God's. Only when we surrender our will to God—including our thoughts—can our hearts offer Him genuine worship. We must humble ourselves before God and give Him all our devotion, not just an unoccupied corner of our minds. Our minds might wander to our own interests, but as soon as we realize that is happening we can repent and refocus. As we concentrate on our Almighty God, we see our unworthiness.

True worship changes us, giving us new goals in life so we desire to please God and not ourselves. All our thoughts, words, and actions should glorify God. That is true worship. Only when self has given up the heart's throne can a person offer God pure worship, unhindered by distractions.

Have you sincerely worshiped God today? Has it changed your life? Has your love and awe of God increased?

Dear Lord, I want to worship you with all my heart, always giving you first place. Forgive me for thinking of myself too often. I offer myself to you for your honor and glory. In Jesus' name, Amen.

God Himself is present,
Let us now adore Him,
And with awe appear before Him!
God is in His temple,
All within keep silence,
Prostrate lie with deepest reverence.

—Gerhard Tersteegen

The Love of Money

"I aim to be a millionaire by the time I'm thirty-five."

The young man whom I heard saying this centers his life around this goal. His desire for money takes precedence over everything and everyone.

Money offers a false sense of security. Some wealthy people live as paupers, hoarding their money, afraid to relinquish that which they look to for refuge. Behind the desire to be rich, we find a person who wants to be somebody in the eyes of the world. He may think accumulating riches is the way to prove his worth.

The Biblical term "mammon" refers to wealth one regards as a god, or uses for an evil influence. Money is not evil in itself, but loving it and misusing it is wrong.

Paul offers a strong warning about our attitude toward wealth: "But they that will be rich fall into temptation and a snare, and into many foolish and hurtful lusts, which drown men in destruction and perdition. For the love of money is the root of all evil: which while some coveted after, they have erred from the faith, and pierced themselves through with many sorrows" (1 Timothy 6:9–10).

If gaining money at any cost is our goal, we may sell our soul in the process. Lust for money causes dishonesty—deceitful business practices that hurt others and mar our Christian witness to the world. What if we do heap up millions of dollars? We cannot take a penny of it with us into the next world. How much better to pursue a godly life and to experience contentment as we seek true riches!

Rather than making wealth our life goal, let us "follow after righteousness, godliness, faith, love, patience, meekness" (1 Timothy 6:11). These things will draw us closer to God. Earthly wealth cannot buy us eternal life. How much better to be poor and a servant of the Lord than to trust in uncertain and fleeting riches!

> *Dear Lord, please help me keep money in its proper place,*
> *using it for good, and honoring you as my Provider. I*
> *want to love you more than anything else.*
> *In Jesus' name, Amen.*

If I gained the world, but lost the Savior,
Were my life worth living for a day?
Could my yearning heart find rest and comfort
In the things that soon must pass away?[b]

—Anna Olander

[b] Found in *The Christian Hymnary* and *Hymns of the Church.*

My Money or God's?

His acreage had produced bumper crops that year, and he surveyed his heaped up grain with satisfaction. Harvest was still in progress, and his barns were already full. So he planned to build a bigger barn and tear down his old ones (Luke 12:16–20).

The farmer in Jesus' parable never considered that his bounty could feed the poor who lived all around him, or be sold to build homes for the homeless. His greedy spirit thought only of himself and the ease and pleasure riches could give him. Likely he went to bed dreaming about drawing up a blueprint for grander outbuildings. Unfortunately, his life ended that night.

If we think what we have is ours and neglect to ask God to direct our decisions, we follow in the footsteps of this farmer. In Luke 12:21, God calls a person a fool who lays up treasure for himself and is not rich toward God. Covetousness is a sin, and sin separates us from God. When we tolerate sin, it hinders our fellowship with God until we repent. Satan tempts us to rebel. "Why can't I be in control of 'my' possessions?" We must humble ourselves and seek God's forgiveness. How dare we withhold what is rightfully His?

If we use our money to impress others, we are trying to rob God of His glory and take it for ourselves. As Paul tells us in 1 Corinthians 4:7, everything we have we received from God, so why do we glory as if we did it all ourselves? We don't take pride in a gift someone has given us;

we know we didn't have anything to do with it. Likewise, our money and possessions are gifts from God, so He deserves the recognition.

As we release our grip on all we think of as ours, we find God is more precious than ever before. Now our trust is truly in God, not in ourselves or "our" possessions. Our hearts find peace, knowing God will provide all we need—though not necessarily all we want.

Let us remember that as children of God, we are not our own. We are bought with the highest price—Christ's own body and blood. Therefore, we are instructed to "glorify God in your body and in your spirit, which are God's" (1 Corinthians 6:20). All we have and are is a gift from God.

Do you look at your money as yours or God's? Are you being a good steward, faithfully distributing what God has entrusted to you?

Dear Lord, thank you for blessing me. Help me to be a good steward, faithfully using your resources in a way that pleases you. In Jesus' name, Amen.

Where is your heart, dear friend, today?
    Which treasure do you love?
The mammon of this passing world,
    Or riches stored above?
Upon the altar lay your all,
    And God will help you share
With needy souls; they'll see in you
    A Father's love and care.

Worship God Through Giving

King David told God, "Both riches and honour come of thee, and thou reignest over all; and in thine hand is power and might; and in thine hand it is to make great, and to give strength unto all" (1 Chronicles 29:12). David recognized that what we have comes from God's hand; thus, it belongs to Him. We glorify our great God when we offer Him our devoted obedience and trust, giving joyfully back to Him by sharing with others. In giving, we worship. Those who spend money foolishly, hoard it, or give it grudgingly are worshiping at the altar of self.

God wants our unswerving love. This is the best offering we can give him. If He has our hearts, He will also have our finances. We have heard the saying that when we lay ourselves on the altar, we must put our pocketbook there too. We should see ourselves as merely caretakers of His riches, rather than owners.

We need to be openhanded with God's money, using it to help others as we are able. The pull to acquire earthly things fades as we find joy in helping others, giving first through our church, and then to other needs. 1 John 3:17 calls us to examine ourselves: "But whoso hath this world's good, and seeth his brother have need, and shutteth up his bowels of compassion from him, how dwelleth the love of God in him?" How we give can be a gauge of how much we love God. Christ showed compassion for others. We can do no less.

Will you draw near to God today, and worship Him as Lord of all, yes, even of your finances?

With joy we'll open wide our hands;
In love we'll give as He commands;
His blessings shall descend on those
Whose hearts and hands are never closed.

Praise or Pout?

Sister Erma's wrinkled face never glowed more than it did when she was talking about her Jesus. In spite of the heartaches in her life, her praise never stopped. She loved to recount the kindness of her precious Lord. Every time I met her at church she had a new story to tell of God's goodness to her.

King David wrote in Psalm 108:1–3 that he would awake early to praise God. What a good example to follow! When we oversleep, we usually wake up feeling grumpy because we are already late for something. We complain and grumble about our trials or inconveniences, and forget the blessings we have. Instead, set the tempo for the day by beginning it early with worship. You will find it harder to pout after meeting God in prayer and praise.

Do you sometimes feel God isn't as close as He used to be? Do you wonder if He really cares about what you are going through? Try praise. Praise God for His mercy, for His love so great that He sent His Son to die for us. Praise Him for His daily care. Praise God as our great Creator.

Praise God when you're happy. Praise Him when life's burdens overwhelm you. Praise Him when your heart is breaking in sorrow, and when it is overflowing with joy. Never stop praising God. To borrow C. S. Lewis' expression, praise is "mental health made audible."[2] As we offer God our love and devotion, we enjoy deeper fellowship and richer pleasure in His awesome presence. And we can't help praising Him whom we enjoy! We recognize our unworthiness, and we love Him more.

Praise draws us close to the heart of God. The psalmist wrote in Psalm 106:2, "Who can utter the mighty acts of the LORD? Who can show forth all his praise?" We will praise God through all eternity, and never be done praising Him. Great is the Lord!

Dear Lord, I draw near to you today with a heart full of gratitude and praise. May my heart and lips never cease to praise you. Thank you, Lord, for drawing near to me too. In Jesus' name, Amen.

Our lips can only try to give
    The praise which God deserves;
Yet we shall strive with tongue and deed
    Through all life's twists and curves.

Then in the place prepared for us,
    Our song will never end;
Our voices strong will praise the Lord,
    And with the angels blend.

Sing Unto the Lord

*T*he voices of the children seated in the front row rang out: "Yes, Jesus loves me! Yes, Jesus loves me. Yes, Jesus loves me! The Bible tells me so." We smiled at their enthusiasm, but shouldn't we sing likewise with heartfelt happiness? When the Lord sets us free from the bondage of sin, joy springs up within us and flows outward in praise! Proofs of His greatness surround us. How can we be silent?

When God delivered the fleeing Hebrew multitude by engulfing their enemies in the Red Sea, they sang His praise: "The LORD is my strength and song, and he is become my salvation: he is my God, and I will prepare him an habitation; my father's God, and I will exalt him" (Exodus 15:2). Are we rejoicing in our deliverance? Our joy should be expressed in song.

Psalm 149:1 says to sing a new song unto the Lord, and to praise Him in the congregation of the saints. The writer urges us to sing individually and corporately. What does he mean by a new song? Note the Exodus account referenced above: when God effected a new deliverance for His people, they praised Him with a new song. Matthew Henry suggests that singing with "new affections" makes our song new, even if we have sung the words before.[3] When God has our devotion and love, a new song is always springing forth. A song we have known for years feels fresh when we connect with a verse in a deeper way.

Do the songs you sing inspire you to a closer relationship with God?

The world's songs promote sin and self, and pull us away from the path of holiness. They excite our emotions but don't inspire us to deeper worship.

May our songs be those which glorify our Redeemer and Lord, sung with rekindled devotion. Sing, sisters, sing!

Dear Lord, I want to sing a new song of gratefulness and praise, and to shun things that pull me away from you.
In Jesus' name, Amen.

A song of gratitude I raise
    To bless the Lord above
Who brought me from the depths of sin,
    And showered me with love.

A song of thankfulness I lift,
    For I was doomed to die,
Then Christ reached down in love to save,
    And drew me to His side.

A song of humbleness I breathe
    For I unworthy am
Of all the Lord has done for me;
    I praise the sinless Lamb.

Phone Line to God

"Thanks so much for calling, Dad. It's so good to hear your voice. Glad for your encouragement too. Love you. Talk to you soon."

As Susan laid down the phone, she frowned. An uncomfortable thought niggled her mind. *"And when will I hear from you, Susan?"*

"I know it's been a while, Lord, but I've been so busy. There's hardly time in the morning, and with the children . . . I love you, Lord, but I have so little time even for myself." Susan sighed. She knew her excuses sounded flimsy.

"Right now the house is quiet," the Lord seemed to whisper.

Dropping to her knees, Susan cried out to God for forgiveness. Soon a sweet peace stole over her soul. "Thank you, Lord. I really have missed you. I'll start getting up earlier in the morning. I'll begin the day right with a visit with you."

Prayer is our phone line to God. Do we use it frequently? Are we eager to talk to our heavenly Father? Are we listening to His words of encouragement or His kindly reproof? Jesus went out alone to pray to His Father. Then how much more do we mortals need to pray and draw close to God! As we come to God in prayer, we will find our hearts reaching out to others, praying for their needs as well. Praying for one another unites believers as one in Christ.

When the disciples asked Jesus to teach them how to pray, He gave them a model prayer we call the Lord's Prayer (Matthew 6:9–13). Prior to this Jesus had been talking about not praying for show, but communing with God in private. We don't need to use eloquent words, just humbly bring our needs and our praise to God. Our prayers must come from our hearts, expressing our burdens and joys in sincerity. Our loving Father wants to hear from us. And He answers. Let us join in heartfelt prayer, my dear friends! It is our lifeline to God.

Dear heavenly Father, I want to use my phone line to you more often. Forgive me. I know I need that connection with you. Thank you for your loving patience.
In Jesus' name, Amen.

When tests and trials weigh me down,
    I need to stop and pray;
The Lord will hear my humble cry
    When, trusting, I obey.

Choices and Outcomes

$\mathcal{I}$ rubbed my eraser across the grid with firm, hard strokes. I had nearly completed the Sudoku puzzle, only to realize I had chosen wrong. Those numbers I had painstakingly arranged—I had to erase them all and start over. My wrong choice had botched the outcome of the puzzle.

Though frustrating, a bungled Sudoku is only trivial. But how sad to come to the end of a day and realize we have chosen wrong. We're not where we wanted to be. The decisions we make throughout each day affect the outcome of our lives. Putting off devotions until a more convenient time may leave us unprepared for what could happen later that day—dealing with a fussy baby, a flat tire, or upsetting news. Our response might not be the Christlike one we would wish.

Even our shopping choices are important. Does the clothing or fabric we select suit a chaste Christian woman? As in the puzzle, each choice leads to the next step we take. Our choices take us closer to or farther away from God.

Stop today and look at the bigger picture. Ask, "Where am I going? What direction do I want to go? What does the Bible say about the choices I have already made? Am I out of line with the Word of God and its principles? Have my choices drawn me closer to God, or have they encouraged me to go my own way?"

If our choices have taken us in a wrong direction, we can turn around by asking God's forgiveness. Seeking His direction, we can make choices that will lead us home to God.

In Psalm 143:8, David asks God to show him the way to walk. He realized he could not make right choices on his own. We, too, need to rely on God's Word and His Holy Spirit to walk in truth and holiness.

Dear Lord, thank you for forgiving me when I sin.
Help me to make choices that bring me closer to you.
In Jesus' name, Amen.

Each choice we make decides the road
    Our feet will walk today;
Are we on paths He's called us to,
    Or have we lost our way?

Blockage in the Line

"I'm afraid you have some blockage in the arteries of your heart." The surgeon's words echoed off the hard white walls of the examining room. My father and sister had both died from heart attacks, but I felt a strange calm in my heart even as I received this dire news. Several days later I underwent a quadruple bypass surgery. It took a major operation to restore the flow of blood through my heart.

Even as the internal pressure I felt over my heart warned me of a potentially serious problem, so the Holy Spirit speaks to me, reminding me of my commitment to Christ. Ignoring the Spirit's guidance puts my soul at risk in the same way that ignoring the surgeon's counsel would have threatened my physical life.

Do you feel pressure on your spiritual 'heart'? How is the flow of communication with your heavenly Father? Are you enjoying a close relationship with Him, or are there things in your life hindering your fellowship with God? You dare not allow that vital line to become clogged.

The enemy of your soul will bring temptations. Giving in to those temptations means that plaque begins to build up on the arteries of your communication with God. It may be as simple as thinking, *I'm too busy for devotions this morning,* yet you never seem to find time later. Maybe you give in to your flesh and allow your thoughts to drift into ungodly daydreams or fantasies. Perhaps you justify yourself by comparing yourself with others: "At least I don't do the things she does!" Pride rears up its ugly head. Covetousness or the love of money will pull us from the faith and bring us much sorrow. Paul says in 1 Timothy 6:11, "But thou, O man of God, flee these things; and follow after righteousness, godliness, faith, love, patience, meekness."

Is your goal to please your heavenly Father? If so, you will do those things that keep channels open between you and God. Only by keeping open your lifeline with God can you survive and thrive.

> *Dear heavenly Father, reveal to me the things in my life that clog my connection with you. Please forgive me, and help me to find victory. Remove the plaque so I can enjoy close fellowship with you again. In Jesus' name, Amen.*

Lord, I confess to thee sadly my sin;
All I am tell I thee, all I have been:
Purge thou my sin away,
Wash thou my soul this day;
Lord, make me clean.

Then all is peace and light this soul within;
Thus shall I walk with thee, the loved Unseen;
Leaning on thee, my God,
Guided along the road,
Nothing between.[c]

—Horatius Bonar

[c] "No, Not Despairingly," *Hymns of the Church*, #840.

A Broken and a Contrite Heart

The woman in the pew ahead of me was trembling so violently she could not hold her hymnal. As we sang the invitation song at the close of the revival service, several people responded to the call of Christ. Someone spoke to the woman, but she stubbornly shook her head, even though tears streaked her face.

Pride keeps us from admitting our need of God. We believe we can make it through life on our own. In contrast, brokenness opens our hearts to God. David modeled this posture as he prayed, "Search me, O God, and know my heart: try me, and know my thoughts: and see if there be any wicked way in me, and lead me in the way everlasting" (Psalm 139:23–24).

In Isaiah 57:15, God promises to reside with the humble and to keep him alive: "For thus saith the high and lofty One that inhabiteth eternity, whose name is Holy; I dwell in the high and holy place, with him also that is of a contrite and humble spirit, to revive the spirit of the humble, and to revive the heart of the contrite ones."

Isaiah had a vision of the Lord sitting upon a high throne. He heard seraphim crying, "Holy, holy, holy, is the LORD of hosts: the whole earth is full of his glory" (Isaiah 6:3). At the reality of God's holiness, Isaiah confessed he was undone, unclean, and unworthy. God did not leave him in this state, but sent a seraph to touch his mouth with a live coal from the altar, and to purge his sin. With a humble, purified heart, Isaiah awaited God's direction. When the Lord asked, "Whom shall I send?" Isaiah answered, "Here am I; send me" (Isaiah 6:8).

God is pleased when we admit our sin and are sorry for it. He wants a relationship with us, but His holiness can't be joined with our sinfulness. Have you wept over your sins? Are you willing to humble yourself before God and commit your life to Him?

A broken and a contrite heart is one God can use. This sacrifice pleases God. When we humble ourselves before God, He will bless us.

> *Dear Lord, Forgive me for the pride in my life, for thinking I can make it on my own. I offer you my broken and contrite heart. I yield my life to you today. Thank you for calling me back to you. In Jesus' name, Amen.*

The Lord will bless the humble heart;
The penitential prayer He hears;
His smile is on the heart that yields
In godly sorrow, bathed with tears.

51

Under the Knife

As I left the house of my old school friend, my heart felt heavy with concern. Although my friend was suffering from complications caused by diabetes and needed surgery, her family had told me she refused to "go under the knife." Later I heard that infection had caused her death.

How likely would we be to tolerate even a small area of gangrene in a finger? Most of us would act promptly to cut away that infection! But do we allow things in our lives that will poison our spiritual vitality? We may think our wrongdoing is too insignificant for God to care about or notice. "Little" sins—those we tend to excuse or ignore—can dull our consciences and gradually pull us away from God. Once the devil gains a foothold in our lives, he doesn't want to give it up, but tries to take even more ground. Jesus said Satan comes to steal, kill, and destroy (John 10:10). That poison keeps spreading.

When we have been tempted in a certain weak spot, or if we have succumbed to that temptation, what do we do about it? If we turn our hearts toward God, His Holy Spirit will convict us and show us our need. He may use others to prod us to take spiritual inventory of our lives. Maybe they don't know the specific sin, but they sense we have a need. If we refuse to listen to God and fellow believers, we will die spiritually. We cannot have a close relationship with God unless we ask Him to keep purging away our sin.

In 1 John 3:6 we find the secret to having victory over sin. "Whosoever abideth in him (Jesus) sinneth not." This means we must stay in close fellowship with Him, sharing with Him and listening to His promptings. When we realize Satan is tugging us away from God—the poison of sin slowly spreading its silent, deadly way through our lives—we must immediately cry out to God for help. The name and blood of Jesus Christ put the enemy to flight and make us overcomers.

Won't you allow God to "operate" on you so you can be without spot and blameless, abiding in Him?

Dear Lord, I open my heart to the light of your truth.
Cleanse my heart, so I can be your pure, spotless bride.
In Jesus' name, Amen.

Search me, O God, and know my heart today;
Try me, O Savior, know my thoughts I pray;
See if there be some wicked way in me:
Cleanse me from ev'ry sin and set me free.

—James Edwin Orr

God's Chastening Hand

Terrible screams erupted in the grocery store. A preschooler ahead of us in the checkout lane was begging for candy. His distracted mother tried at first to shush him, but finally gave him what he wanted. I felt sorrier for the boy than the mother; I suspected his parents had neglected to discipline him at home. He had become an expert at getting his way. What heartache this brings!

In contrast, what joy to be around children who have learned proper behavior and self-control. As Proverbs 29:17 says, "Correct thy son, and he shall give thee rest; yea, he shall give delight unto thy soul."

God uses chastening to teach us it is best for us to follow His counsel and laws. Too often we act like children determined to have our way. In Jonah's case, God had to use drastic measures to punish his disobedience. It took three days in the belly of a big fish for Jonah to repent. He promised to obey God's directive to preach to the wicked city Nineveh.

God is pleased when His chastening changes our behavior. Hebrews 12:5–6 says, "My son, despise not thou the chastening of the Lord, nor faint when thou art rebuked of him: for whom the Lord loveth he chasteneth, and scourgeth every son whom he receiveth." Do we appreciate God's love and concern for us? He corrects us to bring us back into fellowship with Him.

Recently I came across a note my daughter wrote when she was in grade school. She had been disobedient and disrespectful, and I had disciplined her. The next day she wrote to thank me for correcting her. She was sorry for her actions and asked for forgiveness. Then she wrote, "I love you. You are the best mom a girl could have." You can see why I treasure that note. Each time I read it, it brings tears to my eyes. How pleased I felt with her response to chastening! Likewise, our heavenly Father rejoices when we repent, change our behavior, and offer Him our respect and love.

Dear heavenly Father, thank you for your chastening when I go astray. I don't want to lose fellowship with you. Forgive me for being willful and choosing my own way. In Jesus' name, Amen.

O Lord, I need your chastening rod
When from your path I stray;
It makes my heart repent and turn
To choose the narrow way.

Death and Grief— Our Teachers

In years gone by the death knell was rung to mark a person's death. It acknowledged a life that had fled and reminded the living of their mortality. The stark certainty of death forced people to consider what is beyond this life.

Death of a dear one changes us for better or worse. How we respond shapes the rest of our lives. We can harbor anger in our hearts until it poisons us. We become unforgiving, unsociable, unloving, and uncaring.

But what does God want us to learn through the pain of grief and death? One lesson is that God loves us. He promises to be our strength and comfort. Another important lesson we learn is to show compassion for others, like Jesus did.

Jesus wept with His friends Mary and Martha as their brother lay dead in the tomb. He called Lazarus from the grave that day, and everyone rejoiced. Someday He will call all those who are His with a trumpet's blast, and we will meet Him in the air. What rejoicing there will be on that great day for every believer! Death will be finally banished for the saints of God. Our sorrow and grief will be laid aside forever. Until then we must allow our sorrow to draw us closer to God.

Death reminds us of how precious life is. Do we cherish those around us? We don't know when that death knell might toll for one of them.

May we also reach out to others who are grieving, and offer them hope in Christ.

> *Dear Lord, I give my grief to you. I trust you will use it to teach me what you want me to learn, and keep me until the day you call me home to yourself.*
> *In Jesus' name, Amen.*

Though here our life is filled with pain,
    Our sorrow hard to bear,
Yet those in Christ have hope to claim;
    My friends, do not despair!

Our God is here to comfort us;
    He sees our every tear.
Let's lay our burdens at His feet
    And rest! The Savior's near.

Abiding in the Vine

While picking the luscious looking grapes in my mother's arbor, I pictured the refreshing glasses of juice we would enjoy. The branches hung full—except for one branch I spied hiding behind the leaves of others. Not a single leaf or cluster of grapes grew from it. Looking closer, I saw it had broken off near the ground. *No wonder it's barren and useless,* I thought. *It's not connected to the vine.*

Jesus compared our relationship with Him to a vine and its branches. A vine rooted in the earth takes in nourishment from the soil and rain. The vascular system within the stem carries sustenance to the branches. In time, branches sprout leaves and bear fruit. If a branch is broken off, it is worthless—except as kindling. It will never bear fruit apart from the vine.

Jesus said, "I am the vine, ye are the branches: he that abideth in me, and I in him, the same bringeth forth much fruit: for without me ye can do nothing" (John 15:5). The only way to be a productive Christian is to be one with Christ. Are we receiving nourishment from the true Vine, Jesus Christ, or have our connections been severed?

John 15:8 tells us that when we bear fruit, we glorify God. Fruit-bearing is expected not only of believers we expect to be extra-spiritual—like ministers or missionaries—but of all who are connected to the Vine.

One proof of our abiding in Christ is the fruit we display. Galatians 5:22–23 lists the fruit of the Spirit which every Christian should be portraying: "love, joy, peace, longsuffering, gentleness, goodness, faith, meekness, temperance." To produce such fruit, we must be connected to Christ.

Remember, Christ is our source of life. We will be fruitful when we are faithful and obedient to Christ. Can others tell we get our nourishment from Him?

Dear Lord, I want to abide in you. Help me to be faithful so I can bear fruit for you. I praise you for giving me life and nourishment. In Jesus' name, Amen.

"I am the vine and ye are the branches;"
Bear precious fruit for Jesus today;
Branches in Him no fruit ever bearing,
Jesus hath said, "He taketh away."

—Knowles Shaw

Puzzle Pieces

wo of Christ's disciples trudged along the road from Jerusalem to Emmaus (Luke 24:13–14). Discouraged, they discussed Jesus' death as they walked. Why hadn't Jesus delivered them from Roman bondage? And what about Mary's astonishing claim, that she had seen Jesus alive? Life felt like a box of puzzle pieces that didn't fit together. Nothing made sense anymore. Would they, too, be captured and tortured? What should they do now?

A stranger approached and asked what they were talking about. They did not recognize Jesus until He blessed the bread at supper and gave it to them (Luke 24:30–31). Though He vanished out of their sight, He left them ecstatic with hope. Christ was alive! Returning to Jerusalem right away, they found the other disciples. I imagine they interrupted each other, trying to share the details of their evening surprise. As they told the doubtful disciples about meeting Jesus, He suddenly appeared among them.

Jesus had come to put life to rights again, to put the pieces together. Assuring them He really was alive, He explained the prophecies of old and gave them clear direction for the future. They were to preach repentance and forgiveness of sins in the name of Jesus to all people, starting in Jerusalem. They were to wait in Jerusalem until He bequeathed the Holy Spirit's power upon them.

Jesus led them out into the countryside, and while He was blessing them, He ascended into heaven (Luke 24:46–51). Despite their sadness at His departure, the disciples now had a sense of purpose. The puzzle pieces had come together; the picture was clear. They had a mission to accomplish with the power of the Holy Spirit.

Does your life feel disjointed, like an impossibly difficult puzzle? Christ still helps make sense of life for those who seek Him. He still has a mission for all of us, and offers His followers the power to accomplish it. If you don't know how to put the pieces into place, let Jesus take over. He is alive! Trust the pieces of your life to Him today. He will fit them together into a picture that pleases Him.

Dear Lord, please help me make sense of my life. I can't manage on my own. I need you and your power to overcome. Thank you. In Jesus' name, Amen.

God moves in a mysterious way His wonders to perform;
He plants His footsteps in the sea, and rides upon the storm.

Judge not the Lord by feeble sense, but trust Him for His grace;
Behind a frowning providence He hides a smiling face.

Blind unbelief is sure to err, and scan His work in vain;
God is His own interpreter, and He will make it plain.

—William Cowper

A Lacy Snare

*J*ust outside my kitchen window, a spider's web glistens in the morning sunshine. Though a beautiful work of art, it serves as a snare to trap insects. The spider waits in the center of the web for prey to bumble into the web's sticky fibers. Venom from the spider's bite kills the prey, and enzymes which the spider injects liquefy the internal organs of the victim, allowing the spider to dine on these juices.[4]

Like the sparkling, glittering spider's web outside the window, Satan spins a web of deceit in front of us. He makes sin look attractive and inviting. Remember, though—he is planning our destruction. When the web of sin has caught and entangled us, the devil will only laugh at our gullibility.

I watched a fly caught in the spider's web. Though it struggled, it could not free itself from the sticky strands. Likewise, when trying in our own strength to resist the devil, we cannot get free. We must cry out to Jesus to deliver us and give us grace to overcome sin.

The children of Israel, even after experiencing a wonderful deliverance from Egypt, had not learned to rely on God's strength to free them. They displeased God by wanting to turn back to the things they had left behind, including evil ways of worship (Exodus 32).

When Christ delivers us from sin, we must not look back longingly at our former life, as Paul exhorted the Galatians: "Stand fast therefore in the liberty wherewith Christ has made us free, and be not entangled again with the yoke of bondage" (Galatians 5:1).

Satan never gives up trying to pull us back into his clutches. Let us be on guard! Even common sense may mislead us. "There is a way that seemeth right unto a man, but the end thereof are the ways of death" (Proverbs 16:25). Don't be deceived by Satan's enticing offers.

Let the fear of God be your safeguard. God promises to be your strength in time of trouble and to save you as you trust in Him (Psalm 37:39–40). Don't be deceived by the tempter, but cling to Jesus and walk in the light of His truth.

> *Dear Lord, help me keep my eyes on you so that I will not*
> *be enticed into sin and entangled in Satan's web.*
> *In Jesus' name, Amen.*

The spider spins a web so fine
To lure its helpless prey;
And Satan sets a snare for us;
Be watchful every day.

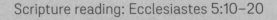

An Insatiable Appetite

"My mouth is still hungry, but my stomach is full." My young grandson pushed his chair back from my kitchen table, a look of regret on his face. He eyed the peanut butter pie longingly, yet he knew he had eaten enough.

Many people pursue their hearts' desires with an insatiable appetite, grasping for pleasure, power, or popularity—and never finding enough. The lust of the flesh is never satisfied, it always craves more. The more a person "eats," the more he will desire: "All the labour of man is for his mouth, and yet the appetite is not filled" (Ecclesiastes 6:7). Sometimes we convince ourselves that it's okay to yield to sin just one more time and then we'll stop, but our uncontrolled and unsatisfied appetite drives us on.

King Solomon, the wisest man on earth, lost his focus later in life when he turned his heart away from God and sought the pleasures of the world. Soon he began worshiping idols. Instead of finding joy in the Lord, he found life empty and fruitless. He had it all, had done it all, so what was left but to die? Even contemplating death gave him no hope, for what hope exists without God?

But thanks be to God! What glorious hope He offers us! Jesus satisfies our longings, and gives us new, holy desires: "Therefore if any man be in Christ, he is a new creature: old things are passed away; behold, all things are become new" (2 Corinthians 5:17).

Romans 6:11–13, 22 show how we are to live our new life in Christ. We are to be dead to sin, but alive unto God through Jesus Christ our Lord. As we yield ourselves to God, He gives us power to live victorious over sinful appetites so we can serve Him joyfully. And He promises us not only a triumphant life now, but also an eternal future with our Savior.

Do you crave the things of God? If not, won't you seek Christ today? He satisfies the hungry soul (Psalm 107:9).

Dear Lord, thank you for satisfying me, and for the new life I have in you. Help me to keep my focus on you, so I can live to please you. In Jesus' name, Amen.

The one who walks with Christ each day
    Makes pleasing God his aim
And finds in Him his longings filled—
    Which glorifies His name.

Truth We Can Rely On

How readily do you believe what you hear? Whether you hear a juicy bit of gossip or come across made-up news on the Internet, it takes discernment to sort out truth from falsehood. Lies abound. God's Word, in contrast, merits our complete trust, for it is complete truth (John 17:17).

Our society disregards God's Word, banning it from schools and public buildings, demoting it to the level of common literature. Even those who claim to believe that the Bible is God's Word manipulate its words to make it say what they want to hear. Yet it endures, as the psalmist testified: "Thy word is true from the beginning: and every one of thy righteous judgments endureth for ever" (Psalm 119:160).

Jeremiah warned God's people of prophets who by their false prophecies and dreams caused the people to err (Jeremiah 23). Unfortunately, Satan can still use those who claim to be God's ministers to lead people astray. We need to beware of false teachings, of people who claim God didn't actually mean what He said. What God calls sin will always be sin regardless of what the law allows or society practices. Do not be deceived!

The best way to avoid deception is to cling to God's pure Word. Be very familiar with Scripture. Live by its principles every day. Stand for Christ, "That ye may be blameless and harmless, the sons of God, without rebuke, in the midst of a crooked and perverse nation, among whom ye shine as lights in the world" (Philippians 2:15). Let His light of truth shine through you, dispelling deception.

Dear Lord, help me cling to your Word, to live by it, and be ready to suffer or die for your truth. Thank you for dying for me so I can live forever. In Jesus' name, Amen.

The Word of God cannot be changed,
　　Its truth fore'er will stand;
Though some men still reject His Word,
　　Ignoring His command.

We must believe in Christ the Lord,
　　Be faithful to the end.
The Word of God will judge us right;
　　On Christ we can depend.

Woe comes to those who try to change
　　The Word of God divine!
Their judgment shall be swift and sure;
　　God's truth surpasses time.

One Body, One Lord

Usually when people are converted but have no church home, they are encouraged to find a solid, Biblical congregation with whom to worship and belong. Why is this important? You might ask, "Can't I serve the Lord and worship alone, or with just my family?" Perhaps you can to some extent, depending on the circumstances, but God knows we need the body of Christ. Our Scripture reading points out that all members in the body of Christ are needed, even necessary, for the body's spiritual wellbeing.

Christ is the head of His spiritual body, the church. Just as your brain controls the members of your body, so Christ controls His church. Without the head, the body cannot function properly, nor even live. As the members of your physical body work together to help each other, we, as the body of Christ, are to encourage and support one another. When one is hurting, we are to comfort and to bind up her wounds. Ephesians 6:18 shows that one way we can do this is by persevering in prayer for each other.

Paul gave thanks for the church at Thessalonica because their faith and love for one another abounded (2 Thessalonians 1:3). Like water does for our physical bodies, love is the "oil" that lubricates each member so the body will work together smoothly. Without that love, friction or irritation can occur when people work closely together.

As believers we have not only accountability to Christ, but also to our brothers and sisters in the faith. God's will is for us to work together as one body, obeying Christ our head. Then we can joyfully come together to celebrate our oneness in Christ as we remember His suffering, death, and resurrection. One with each other, and one in Christ is the closeness God wants us to experience. The body of Christ cares not only for our physical wellbeing, but especially for our spiritual health. May we each do our part to support, love, comfort, and encourage one another.

Dear Lord, thank you for your Church, and for the help each member is to me. Help me to be open to the counsel of the body, to accept their concern for me. I know this is to help me draw closer to you. Lord, use me to encourage others. Thank you for the oneness we have in you, our head. In Jesus' name, Amen.

Through Christ's dear blood, He made us one;
O may we serve our Head, the Son.
To prove our love and gratefulness,
We'll nurture all with carefulness.

Who Has Your Heart?

Cindy turned off her light and climbed into bed, but not to sleep. She couldn't get the words of the evangelist out of her mind. "Who has your heart? Your actions prove if it is God or Satan. Do you seek God's approval before making decisions, or do you think, 'It's my right to choose what I do?'"

But I'm a pretty good person, Cindy thought. *I don't do bad things. I go to church more than most young people my age. I even pay my tithe. Why can't I decide who I will date or marry, or how I will dress, and where I will go? Why do my parents have to place so many restrictions on what I do? I'm mature and responsible. Do I have to ask God about everything?*

The Spirit of God gently nudged Cindy. *"Who has your heart, Cindy? If you want to rule, there is no place for Christ."* Stunned and ashamed, repentant tears began to slip down Cindy's cheeks. She prayed, "O Lord, forgive me. I was wrong, and full of pride. I want you to abide and rule in my heart. I can't trust my judgment, but must lean on yours. Thank you for loving me, and showing me where I was headed."

Who holds your heart, dear reader? What is standing in your way of making a full commitment to Christ? Verse 34 of today's reading says, "For where your treasure is, there will your heart be also." Is your heart fully surrendered to Jesus? Do you love Him with all your heart, mind, and soul? Is Christ your treasure?

God knows what we need and what is best for us. He wants us to seek the things of God and live for His glory. There we will find true happiness.

Are you ready to surrender all to Christ, making him Lord of your life? If you want to be with Him forever, Christ must have your heart today.

Dear Jesus, I want to love you more than anything else. Help me to daily lay down self, so nothing will claim my heart but you alone. In Jesus' name, Amen.

With all the heart, the soul, the might,
　　I'll love the Lord each day,
And keep this heart where Christ abides
　　A place He'll want to stay.

Staying Within God's Parameters

Our puppy enjoyed running free while my husband did chores, until one day he crossed our property line. He ignored our calls, and the neighbor children chased him home, their own dog adding his fierce barks. Now our puppy remains on a leash. He forfeited his freedom when he disobeyed.

Do we Christians ever feel frustrated by God's boundaries? Do we strain at the leash, wanting to run free? Throughout the Bible God sets conditions we must meet to have His approval. Disobedience brings His displeasure. God doesn't want to be mean or make things hard for us. He wants to protect us from the awful consequences of sin.

Running free is not all it appears to be. Ignoring God's rules, making our own way in life, we are like helpless children turned loose in a strange city to find our way home alone.

Today's women are encouraged to be bold and free of constraints, regardless of the cost to their families and spiritual lives. As godly women, we have a different purpose. First, to love God with all our hearts. Second, to love, obey, and honor our authorities, whether husband, father, employer, or church leaders. Third, to cherish and nurture the children in our lives, guiding them in the fear of the Lord.

Do the parameters set for us seem too confining? Do we feel the urge to spread our wings and fly away? Are we like children wanting to explore where it isn't safe? Are we floundering around, trying to find our way, taking off into dangerous territory because it looks attractive? God wants us to stay close to Him. Our souls are precious to Him, so precious that He gave His Son to die for us.

Yearning after so-called freedom brings dissatisfaction in our Christian life. Instead, let us embrace with thanksgiving the parameters God has given us. As we listen to His voice and obey, we won't feel the need to explore forbidden territory. We will find we have all we need within God's boundaries. We are truly free when we submit.

Dear Lord, forgive me for wanting my own way. Help me see the dangers and the consequences I face when I listen to the enemy. I know that in you alone I have true liberty. In Jesus' name, Amen.

Beyond the fence are dangers great;
   We're safe by Jesus' side;
We need to trust His loving hand,
   Within His grace abide.

The Righteous in This Generation

How does our generation compare with Noah's? The wickedness of Noah's generation grieved the heart of God (Genesis 6:5–6). They thought only of evil continually. When God saw how they had turned against Him, He was sorry He had created man and placed him on earth. God could have wiped out *all* the creatures living on land, but He saw Noah and his family. The Bible calls Noah a just and perfect man who found grace in God's eyes. Because of Noah's fidelity, God preserved him and his family when He covered the whole earth with a flood.

How many righteous does God see in this generation? Proverbs 14:34 tells us, "Righteousness exalteth a nation: but sin is a reproach to any people." Those who say, "There is no God" refuse to acknowledge a holy God because of their own evil deeds and hearts. Yet their sin brings consequences. Galatians 6:7–8 warns us: "Be not deceived; God is not mocked: for whatsoever a man soweth, that shall he also reap. For he that soweth to his flesh shall of the flesh reap corruption; but he that soweth to the Spirit shall of the Spirit reap life everlasting."

In a world where He is hardly acknowledged, God still sees the faithful and true who walk in righteousness. He hears their fervent prayers (James 5:16), but "the face of the Lord is against them that do evil" (1 Peter 3:12).

"All have sinned, and come short of the glory of God" (Romans 3:23), but we have the promise "if we confess our sins, he is faithful and just to forgive us our sins, and to cleanse us from all unrighteousness" (1 John 1:9). Through faith in Christ who shed His blood for us, we are justified, and He clothes us with a robe of righteousness, pure and clean. Is your robe still that way, or has it become spotted with the things of this world?

Are you among those God sees as righteous in this generation? Are you ready for Christ's coming? Are you a light to those who sit in darkness today?

Dear Lord, help me to abide in you so I can shine in the darkness of this world and be ready for your return. Thank you for clothing me with your righteousness, and giving me eternal life. In Jesus' name, Amen.

Are you washed in the blood?
　Have you been redeemed?
Are you wearing a robe
　That is spotlessly clean?

Rewards of the Righteous

"Earn more rewards faster!" The bold letters on the credit card advertisement slid out of my sight and into the trash bin. Rewards. How they excite us! Children may earn them for doing chores on time without complaining. Students may earn them if they have no demerits or absences. In the workplace, employees may receive them for years of service. Some stores offer reward points for dollars spent. None of these begin to compare, however, with the rewards Christ wants to give us.

In the examples above, conditions must be met before rewards are given. Christ, too, has conditions for the rewards He offers. The first is that we believe Christ is the Son of God, and that He came to earth to die for us. Another condition is that we confess our sins, after which He says we become children of God. Jesus also promises eternal life to those who believe in Him (John 3:16).

We need not wait for heaven to enjoy many of Christ's rewards. Believing in Christ fills us with joy (1 Peter 1:7). Christ promised peace to His disciples: "Peace I leave with you, my peace I give unto you: not as the world giveth, give I unto you. Let not your heart be troubled, neither let it be afraid" (John 14:27). Because we belong to Him, He fills us with a peace this world can neither offer nor take from us.

Jesus asks us to be holy, obedient, and faithful, and He promises to help us. God's blessing rests on those who hear the Word of God and obey it (James 1:25).

1 John 4:16 says, "And we have known and believed the love that God hath to us. God is love; and he that dwelleth in love dwelleth in God, and God in him." What a blessed reward to experience such closeness with God!

Rewards await those who remain steadfast under trial: "Be thou faithful unto death, and I will give thee a crown of life" (Revelation 2:10). We will sit with Jesus on His throne (Revelation 3:21). We will have no more tears, death, or sorrow. The greatest reward, however, is to be with our Savior forever. Don't miss the rewards here and in the future!

Dear Lord, by your grace I want to be faithful and rejoice in your blessings. In Jesus' name, Amen.

God loves to bless His children,
   Rewarding work well done,
But best of all is knowing
   We'll dwell with God's own Son.

Where Is Your Name Written?

Have you ever written your name on a sandy beach? Perhaps you built elaborate castles or long roads. When you went back the next day, what did you find? The waves had washed the sand smooth, leaving no trace of your creativity.

Jesus rebuked His disciples because they rejoiced that the devils were subject to them through His name. He said, "Rather rejoice, because your names are written in heaven." (Luke 10:20)

Do we want to make a name for ourselves? Are we tempted to be proud of our gifts? God blesses us when we use them for Him, but we have no right to become proud. After all, we must remember God has given us any talents or gifts we possess (1 Corinthians 4:7). Though men might praise us or write about our accomplishments, their acclaim will vanish like writing in the sand.

Revelation 21 describes the holy city prepared for those who belong to Christ, where only the redeemed may enter: "And there shall in no wise enter into it any thing that defileth, neither whatsoever worketh abomination, or maketh a lie: but they which are written in the Lamb's book of life" (v. 27). When our names are written there, the crashing waves of trouble can't wash them out!

God is calling us today to come to Him, find forgiveness for our sins, and have our names written in the Lamb's book of life. Is your name recorded there? Then you can look forward to living in the very presence of Christ in the holy city with all who believe in Him.

Remember, all Satan offers you—wealth, prestige, honor—will perish. Only Christ can offer you eternal life. Only Christ has the power to transform your life, and write your name in His book.

Dear Lord, I want my name to be written in your book of life. Help me to be faithful to you, to obey your Word, and to be ready to enter into that glorious city that you have prepared for your own. In Jesus' name, Amen.

Is my name written there
On the page white and fair?
In the book of Thy kingdom,
Is my name written there?

—Mary A. Kidder

79

Scripture reading: Psalm 142:1–7

Through Afflictions

Arvella stared out the window, but tears blurred her vision. "So many tears these days! It has been months since Roger's death. Why can't I get over this grief? So many things remind me of him. All I have now is lonely days and nights." Turning from the window, she clasped her Bible to her heart. "Oh, God! Be my comforter today. I know you have not forsaken me, but grief threatens to overwhelm me. Give me strength to go on and find a purpose in life. I don't want to drown in my tears."

Like Arvella, the psalmist knew where to turn to in affliction, for he testified, "Trouble and anguish have taken hold on me: yet thy commandments are my delights" (Psalm 119:143). Afflictions reveal our need of God. King David knew all about this. On numerous occasions he had to run for his life. He bore the blame for the death of his infant son, God's judgment for David's immorality. Another son tried to wrest the kingdom from him. He felt forsaken by friends, and he even felt God was hiding His face from him. Yet again and again David cried out to the Lord, reminding himself that his only hope and refuge is in God.

When our good health deteriorates, and pain is our constant companion, to whom do we turn? Is God our strength and hope? Reminded of our mortality, we must fix our hearts on God and the home He is preparing for us. Life is never without trials, but in the midst of them, we are not alone. Jesus will never leave us. If we feel estranged from

Him, it is we who have stepped away. Every day we must choose to draw nearer to Him.

Can we learn from our trials and afflictions, and use that knowledge to help others? Can we praise God when we are going through difficulty? God's Word offers hope and comfort. Draw close to God, and He will draw close to you (James 4:8). Remember, He understands our feelings because He has experienced them (Hebrews 4:15).

Dear Lord, through joys or sorrows I want to draw closer to you. Use the afflictions of life to purify and refine me, making me a vessel you can use. In Jesus' name, Amen.

When the trials of life
    Rob the joy in your soul,
Trust the great King who reigns;
    He is still in control.
All these troubles will pass
    When our journey is o'er.
Then we'll rest in our home,
    Praise the Lord we adore.

Salvation and Song

"Reproach hath broken my heart; and I am full of heaviness: and I looked for some to take pity, but there was none; and for comforters, but I found none" (Psalm 69:20). These words of the psalmist carry prophetic overtones, describing Christ's humiliation. Perhaps to some degree you, too, have hit rock bottom spiritually, physically, and/or emotionally. It feels as though our song is gone. In these most vulnerable moments, Satan tries to attack us. He wants us to doubt our salvation and to feel God has forsaken us. We must not believe his lies.

Loving, kind, longsuffering, and merciful—God reveals Himself as all of these. If we cry out to Him, He lifts us out of the pit of despair. He has promised to never forsake us, and God keeps his promises. Even if we sin, He offers forgiveness when we repent in godly sorrow. God never pushes away the repentant heart or the needy, seeking soul. Our Father delights in giving us good gifts, replacing our sorrow with joy, and bringing peace to our soul in the midst of turmoil and strife. He promises to give us a new song (Psalm 40:3).

David testified, "I called upon the LORD in distress: the LORD answered me, and set me in a large place" (Psalm 118:5). Satan wants to confine us, even bind us with chains. He makes us feel trapped, unable to escape his snares. God sets us free and puts us in a place where we can serve Him. God is on our side! Why should we worry or fear?

Like the psalmist, we, too, can trust God for deliverance from sin and despair. We can say with him, "The LORD is my strength and song, and is become my salvation" (Psalm 118:14). God doesn't tire of listening to His children. He wants us to depend upon Him and to praise Him even in the darkness. He knows we lack the strength to face all the struggles of life alone. His waiting ears hear our faintest call. Will you cry out to Him and sing when life seems dark?

Dear Lord, forgive me for doubting you, for believing I have to handle life on my own. Help me to praise you even in the hard times. Thank you for hearing my cry for help and delivering me. I praise you, dear Father, for your great love and mercy. In Jesus' name, Amen.

"O don't be anxious, child of mine,
　　When you are tested sore,
For I am here; you're not alone;
　　So learn to trust me more.

"O look to me, and you will find
　　The strength to persevere.
A grain of faith can mountains move;
　　Your song and cry I hear."

Grace and Truth

My husband and I moved about the huge hospital ward, stopping here and there to chat with the patients. When we asked if they were ready to meet God, they responded in different ways. Some could hardly wait to see the Lord. Others shrugged, saying, "Oh, I'm not too worried. I've heard God is a God of love and mercy, and I'm a pretty good person. I think I'll be okay." Those people presumed upon God's mercy even though they had not placed their trust in Christ.

God *is* a God of love and mercy. That love and mercy moved Him to send His only Son Jesus to this world to die for us. He made a way for us to be right with Him, to have our sins forgiven, and to be reconciled to our Creator. That way is Jesus Christ, His Son.

The Son is not only the way; He is also the truth (John 14:6). Obedience to His Word is necessary if we expect to receive His promised heaven. Merely calling Him "Lord" does not mean we have entered His kingdom if we go on living in disobedience to His will (Matthew 7:21–27). We cannot ignore God's Word and His Son's sacrifice for us, and expect mercy after death. We must acknowledge our sinfulness and our need of a Savior. Otherwise we will not find mercy when we face God.

Grace isn't something we ever can earn or deserve. We can't buy it or borrow it. "For by grace are ye saved through faith; and that not of yourselves: it is the gift of God: not of works, lest any man should boast" (Ephesians 2:8–9). Our merciful God saw we needed forgiveness for our sins, and He provided the answer through His Son Jesus, extending His grace as a free gift to all who come to Him. Love motivated this gift: "But God, who is rich in mercy, for his great love wherewith he loved us, even when we were dead in sins, hath quickened us together with Christ, (by grace ye are saved;)" (Ephesians 2:4–5).

"Grace and truth came by Jesus Christ" (John 1:17). God offers no alternate routes to heaven—only Christ. Don't just hope God will accept you. If you have believed on Christ and follow Him, you won't fear death or God's judgment. Instead, you'll anticipate Christ's return.

Will you accept God's grace and claim His truth today?

Dear Lord, be merciful to me a sinner. I want to accept your free gift of grace and salvation, and trust you for my future. In Jesus' name, Amen.

Marvelous grace of our loving Lord,
Grace that exceeds our sin and our guilt,
Yonder on Calvary's mount outpoured,
There where the blood of the Lamb was spilt.

Marvelous, infinite, matchless grace,
Freely bestowed on all who believe;
You who are longing to see His face,
Will you this moment His grace receive?

—Julia H. Johnston

85

Unfailing Faithfulness

As I reached up to pin another piece of laundry to the clothesline, I noticed the sky. The sight of towering cumulus clouds sailing in a sea of brilliant blue caused me to pause and breathe deeply. My mind went to Psalm 36:5: "Thy mercy, O LORD, is in the heavens; and thy faithfulness reacheth unto the clouds." How easily we consider ourselves self-sufficient, forgetting how much we need God's grace and mercy every day!

Proclaiming God's faithfulness brings glory to Him. Like the psalmist, we should "sing of the mercies of the LORD," declaring His faithfulness to people through all ages (Psalm 89:1).

God's Word is firmly fixed in heaven. It stands sure, unchanging. God's faithfulness extends to all generations. He established the earth, and it stands immovable (Psalm 119:89–91). All God created—this universe of stars, moons, and earth—continues according to His law.

Man often violates God's law. Yet even when we fail to keep His commandments and He needs to chastise us, God promises, "Nevertheless my lovingkindness will I not utterly take from him, nor suffer my faithfulness to fail" (Psalm 89:33). Considering all our failures, "It is of the LORD's mercies that we are not consumed, because his compassions fail not. They are new every morning: great is thy faithfulness" (Lamentations 3:22–23). Even when we falter, we can depend on God; He remains faithful (2 Timothy 2:13). When trials plague us sorely, we must cling to His promise: "There hath no temptation taken you but such as is common to man: but God is faithful, who will not suffer you to be tempted above that ye are able; but will with the temptation also make a way to escape, that ye may be able to bear it" (1 Corinthians 10:13). That promise merits our deepest thankfulness.

When we reflect on all God has done for us—providing salvation through His Son Jesus Christ, blessing us despite our unworthiness, promising us eternal life, making us heirs with Christ—shall we not also be faithful to God?

Dear Lord, I am so glad I can depend on you in every circumstance. Help me, Lord, to be faithful to you, too, and share your faithfulness with others. In Jesus' name, Amen.

Faithful, O Lord, thy mercies are,
A rock that cannot move;
A thousand promises declare,
Thy constancy of love.[5]

—Charles Wesley

87

The Temple of the Lord

Over the years I have listened to my sons discuss their work in construction. They often talked about the importance of doing things the right way to avoid problems later. King David must have shared a similar concern when he passed on explicit instructions to his son Solomon regarding the building and furnishings of the temple. Solomon carefully carried out the construction exactly as his father had directed.

How breathtakingly splendid that temple and its furnishings must have been! Artisans and craftsmen had selected materials of the highest quality to reflect God's glory and honor. The ark of the covenant stood in its place, and the priests, singers, and leaders of the tribes gathered at the east end of the altar to praise the Lord. Finally, the Lord filled His temple with His glory and majesty (2 Chronicles 5).

As new covenant believers, our bodies are the temple of the Holy Ghost who indwells us when we believe in Christ. No longer are we in charge of our lives. Our redemption cost the highest price—the body and blood of God's own Son. Therefore, we ought to glorify God in everything we do (1 Corinthians 6:19–20). We should say nothing, do nothing, go nowhere that would dim the brightness of His light in us.

How is your temple furnished—is it decorated with the beautiful fruits of the Spirit (Galatians 5:22–23)? Is your highest desire to honor God by the things you do, say, or think? Are you offering God your best in time, money, and talents? Ask God to make your temple a glorious place where He dwells in all His majesty.

Dear Lord, I want to honor you in all my ways so you will always dwell in my heart. In Jesus' name, Amen.

Take my life and let it be
    Consecrated, Lord, to Thee;
Take my hands and let them move
    At the impulse of Thy love.

Take my feet, and let them be
    Swift and beautiful for Thee;
Take my voice and let me sing
    Always, only, for my King.

Take my will and make it Thine,
    It shall be no longer mine;
Take my heart, it is Thine own,
    It shall be Thy royal throne.

—Frances Ridley Havergal

Exalt the Lord

What would it have been like to hear God's voice thunder from Mount Sinai as He spoke to His people in the desert (Exodus 20:18)? Today's reading gives us a picture of God's holiness and power as He came down to the mountain with thunder, lightning, smoke, and a trumpet blast to speak to the people. They trembled, fearing this mighty God.

Psalm 99:5 instructs, "Exalt ye the LORD our God, and worship at his footstool; for he is holy." Exalting someone means to praise and honor him. When we exalt the Lord, we go a step further. We allow Him to reign on the throne of our heart. Our words of praise mean nothing if we refuse to make Christ the Lord of our life. Minister Earl Peachy once said, "When a person becomes saved, there is a change of authority in his life. Christ should become the boss."

Do we really want to have control of our own lives, with our eternal destiny at stake? In our flesh we are weak, selfish, and prone to anger and jealousy. When those characteristics motivate our daily decisions, our end will be misery in this world and destruction in the next. Surely it is better to submit our lives to the One who is pure and holy, who is so powerful He uses earth as a footstool (Isaiah 66:1). We exalt the Lord when we allow Him to be the ruler of our lives. We can trust Him to guide our feet in the way they should go. And our future rests securely in His hands.

Such a God deserves all praise! Is this great, holy, and wonderful God ruling as Lord in your life? Examine your heart today and determine to exalt the Lord not only with your mouth, but with your life.

Dear Lord, I ask you to be the Lord of my life. I yield the throne of my heart to you. May you be exalted daily in my life. In Jesus' name, Amen.

Men feared to come before you, Lord,
    You were consuming fire.
None dared approach your holy hill,
    And risk your righteous ire.

And so you sent your Son to earth
    To sinners steeped in sin;
Upon the cross He shed His blood
    To cleanse our hearts within.

Exalted be your holy name!
    We bow our hearts and knees,
And praise you, Lord, for offering us
    Forgiveness full and free.

Confessing Our Faults

"Confess your faults one to another, and pray one for another, that ye may be healed" (v. 16). We find it difficult to own our failures because it forces us to face our sin. It's natural to want others to think well of us, and bringing our sin into the open is humiliating. We fear that God or others will reject us if we really admit what we have done. But hidden sin hurts the body of Christ. It's like a cancer destroying the body, unseen but deadly. We will find ourselves unable to work together well and won't understand why.

Perhaps we have lived as a Christian for many years, but the peace we once had is gone. We try to justify our wrongs, but our excuses and cover-ups, like all lies, come from Satan. We all face different temptations, but they spring from the same source. The devil wants to destroy our relationship with Christ, but Christ wants us to triumph, thus bringing praise and honor to God.

Thank God for convicting us of our faults! He will help us to confess them. This often spurs others to confess theirs. True Christians rejoice at our confession because they want us to have victory. None of us can claim perfection. We all need God's forgiveness and that of our brothers and sisters in Christ.

Confession brings healing, both physical and spiritual. God hears the honest, contrite heart and responds lovingly. Think of a father who sees his toddler fall into the mud. His hand reaches out with compassion, and he quickly offers to clean the child up. God looks at us in much the same way. Confession restores us to fellowship with God and with our brothers and sisters in the Lord.

May we show love and compassion to those who confess their faults, supporting them in prayer and in any other way we can. "Beloved, if God so loved us, we ought also to love one another" (1 John 4:11).

Dear heavenly Father, help me to be willing to confess my faults so I can have victory over sin. Thank you for your love and forgiveness. In Jesus' name, Amen.

It is the little sins which cause
    The greatest saint to fall.
In truth, there is no little sin,
    For God condemns them all.

Confess your sins, and be at peace.
    Rejoice with those who know
Forgiveness from the Lord above,
    And closer to Him grow.

Bringing Hope

The white-haired lady's face glowed as she sang along. A group of us from church were singing at a nursing home, and my eyes were drawn to this woman's face. Her obvious joy inspired me to sing the precious words with more meaning than before.

When I chatted with her later, the elderly woman told me her story. She had never known the Lord before she came to the nursing home. When she heard of the hope He could give her, she repented. "Now I belong to Jesus," she said, "and I am so happy. I can't wait to get to heaven!" Her joy bore witness of her genuine faith. She had hope both for today and the unknown tomorrow.

This woman's confident hope inspires me as I age. When I reach another birthday milestone, I wonder, "What will this year bring?"

Every season of life holds uncertainties, but for older people, troubles can seem especially daunting. Some have no families to support them emotionally or financially. They have many lonely days and wakeful nights, worrying what might happen to them if their money runs out. Poor health can bring its own anxieties. When their own mobility leaves them and increased pain takes its place, discouragement and depression tend to hang over the elderly like a dark cloud.

These earthly bodies will perish, but those who are Christ's look forward to a new body, glorified and whole, that will live forever in the presence of Jesus Christ. What glorious hope! "Now the God of hope fill you with all joy and peace in believing, that ye may abound in hope, through the power of the Holy Ghost" (Romans 15:13).

We are never too old to come to Christ. Placing your hope in the only One who can help you today and eternally will renew your youth like the eagle's (Psalm 103:5). As you face the future, Jesus, our hope, offers to be the anchor of your soul, sure and steadfast (Hebrews 6:19).

Dear Lord, I place my hope in you. I trust you for my future and rejoice in the day you have given me. In Jesus' name, Amen.

Are you worried o'er the future,
    Wond'ring what you'll have to face?
There is blessed hope in Jesus;
    You will ne'er outlive His grace.

Christ the Lord will take our burdens,
    He will calm the troubled soul,
He will offer hope to cheer us
    When we give to Him control.

Bring your burdens all to Jesus,
    And sweet rest your heart will know;
Fears will fade and calm will enter
    When the Lord His peace bestows.

God's People

What heartache Adam and Eve must have felt when their eldest son Cain murdered his brother Abel! This staggering tragedy reminded them anew of the repercussions of their own sin. Later, when their son Seth was born, they believed God was offering them fresh hope in the midst of their grief. Perhaps this son would fear God and teach his family to love Him. From him the Messiah would come. When Seth's son Enos was born, men began to call on the name of the Lord (Genesis 4:26). A marginal reading says, to "call themselves by the name of the Lord."[6] Scholars tell us that idolatry emerged in this time period, so already a separation existed between those who wanted to follow God and those who did not.

This is still true today. We are a called out people, those who serve the Lord, who call upon the name of God. Aligning ourselves with Christ means we yield to His kingship and embrace His authority. Rejection of the world's way of doing things must automatically follow. Not that this will be easy, but it is necessary. The two authorities cannot exist in the same heart; we cannot serve two masters (Matthew 6:24).

Since we are God's people, we conform to His desires, not our own. We count it a privilege to be called the sons and daughters of God. Our lives show that we are not ashamed of our heavenly Father or His Son Jesus Christ who died for us.

Where do you stand today? Do you align yourself with God and His people, or do you follow the path to destruction? God calls each of us to believe on Him and find life eternal. The choice is yours.

> *Dear heavenly Father, thank you for being the great, sovereign God you are. Help me to call upon your name and stand firmly with your people. In Jesus' name, Amen.*

People of the living God,
I have sought the world around;
Paths of sin and sorrow trod,
Peace and comfort nowhere found;
Now to you my spirit turns,
Turns a fugitive unblest;
Brethren, where your altar burns,
Oh, receive me into rest.

—James Montgomery

Bow Down Your Ear

Have you ever bent down to listen to a child? Bringing yourself down to his level encourages him to speak his heart. He feels he really has your attention. Taking time to listen to a child lets him know you care about him.

David prays, "Bow down thine ear, O LORD, hear me: for I am poor and needy" (Psalm 86:1). David wants God to hear him, to listen to the cry of his heart. David's humble posture invites God's presence, for "the LORD is nigh unto them that are of a broken heart; and saveth such as be of a contrite spirit" (Psalm 34:18). The psalmist again pleads with God in desperation when he prays these words: "O LORD God of my salvation, I have cried day and night before thee: let my prayer come before thee: incline thine ear unto my cry" (Psalm 88:1–2).

God not only bowed down His ear to hear humanity's cry for help, He also sent the ultimate remedy—His only Son came to earth to dwell among us and be our Savior.

Unlike some religions where ritual prayers are recited without ever hearing from their god, Christianity offers two-way communication. God told His people, "Incline your ear, and come unto me: hear, and your soul shall live; and I will make an everlasting covenant with you, even the sure mercies of David" (Isaiah 55:3).

Do you feel troubled, afraid, lonely, or discouraged? Remember, "The eyes of the LORD are upon the righteous, and his ears are open unto their cry" (Psalm 34:15). Two verses later we find the same theme: "The righteous cry, and the LORD heareth, and delivereth them out of all their troubles" (Psalm 34:17). Cry out to God in faith. He hears, and He will answer. Seldom will you hear audible words as men did in days of old, but still He answers. It may come through a fellow believer speaking into your life, a verse from His Word coming alive in the quiet of your prayer closet, or a feeling of peace pervading your heart.

Picture the heavenly Father bending His head toward you, listening to the cry of your heart. Then, with your ears attuned to hear, listen to what God wants you to know.

Dear heavenly Father, thank you for hearing my cry for help, for always listening to my problems, for caring about me. Help me, too, to listen to you and to heed your words. In Jesus' name, Amen.

Lord, in the morning thou shalt hear
My voice ascending high;
To thee will I direct my prayer,
To thee lift up mine eye.

—Isaac Watts

God's Sheltering Wings

As a mother of seven, how often I picked up a crying baby, nestled him close to my heart, and soothed him with soft words and kisses. Soon he relaxed, resting in arms of love. His distress melted away when he felt his mother's closeness.

Do you feel alone, uncared for, or afraid? Does unrest or uncertainty weigh you down? Like the baby's crying, our distress should move us to hold our hands up to God. We desperately need His tender care. God longs to comfort His people. But first we must cry out to Him, acknowledging our desire and need for Him.

Our cries will not go unheeded. The psalmist uses the metaphor of a mother hen sheltering her brood to describe God's care: "He shall cover thee with his feathers, and under his wings shalt thou trust" (Psalm 91:4). We will not lack any good thing when we draw near to God. "For he satisfieth the longing soul, and filleth the hungry soul with goodness" (Psalm 107:9).

God does not turn His back to the searching heart. Rather, He opens wide His arms, ready and willing to comfort and embrace the heart longing for God. Jesus says, "Come unto me, all ye that labour and are heavy laden, and I will give you rest (Matthew 11:28).

Whatever your need, wherever you wander, Jesus is calling you to come to Him. He alone can completely satisfy every yearning of your soul.

As mothers, we cannot always comfort our babies; their needs may exceed our ability or knowledge. Our Lord knows us intimately, even seeing into our hearts. He is our Healer, mending broken lives. Jesus satisfies our deepest longing and fills us with His peace.

Nestle under God's protection with perfect trust. Admit your need, and He will draw you close.

Dear Lord, I want to ever rest close to your heart where I am safe and have all I need. Thank you for hearing my cries. In Jesus' name, Amen.

He sees the brokenhearted;
    He hears our fervent pleas;
Our God of great compassion
    Still cares for you and me.

His arms are ever open;
    He longs to hold you near,
To comfort, cheer, and bless you,
    To drive away your fear.

Beautiful Hands

As a child, I would beg my mother to read me the story "Mother's Hands." It told of a young girl who one day noticed the disfiguring scars that covered her mother's hands. Horrified, she blurted out, "Mother, why are your hands so ugly? All my friends' mothers have lovely hands." Her mother's eyes filled with tears, but she drew her daughter near and told her of the day she had rescued her baby girl from a raging house fire, burning her hands severely in the process.

The daughter wept as she clasped her mother's hands and covered them with kisses. "Oh, Mother," she said, "you have the most beautiful hands of all. I will never again think of them as ugly." Hearing her mother's story changed the daughter's perspective, for those hands displayed the cost of her mother's love.[7]

This story reminds me of our Savior's love. His hands, feet, and side were marred—for us. Hanging on a cross, He endured agonizing pain and wore a crown of cruel thorns—for us. He could have come down from the cross or called thousands of angels to rescue Him. But His submission to His heavenly Father and His great love for mankind kept Jesus there on the cross where He laid down His life.

The hands of Jesus still bear the marring scars of the nails. Yet I believe when we see them we will think they are the most beautiful hands we have ever seen, for they tell a story of sacrificial love for us.

Are we longing for the day when we see Christ face to face so we can thank Him again for His saving love?

The Apostle Paul exhorts us to live out this same love today: "Be ye therefore followers of God as dear children; and walk in love, as Christ also hath loved us, and hath given himself for us an offering and a sacrifice to God for a sweet smelling savour" (Ephesians 5:1–2).

> *Dear Lord, I don't deserve your great love. Help me to love as you have loved. Someday I want to clasp your hands that were wounded for me.*
> *In Jesus' name, Amen.*

See, from His head, His hands, His feet,
Sorrow and love flow mingled down;
Did e'er such love and sorrow meet,
Or thorns compose so rich a crown?[d]

—Isaac Watts

[d] "When I Survey the Wondrous Cross," v. 3.

Our God Is So Big

"My God Is So Big." How well I remember the energy with which my children would sing this song! A child's sense of wonder is captivated by a God who is big, mighty, strong, and powerful. A child has no trouble believing that God can do anything. Do we still believe this is true, or do we sometimes doubt He can meet our needs?

Our pride makes us regard ourselves as strong and capable enough to make it through life on our own. What a delusion! Jesus told His disciples, "Without me ye can do nothing" (John 15:5). Similarly, Paul writes, "Not that we are sufficient of ourselves . . . but our sufficiency is of God" (2 Corinthians 3:5). Ephesians 2:8–9 says, "For by grace are ye saved through faith; and that not of yourselves: it is the gift of God: not of works, lest any man should boast." We lack strength, wisdom, and ability—but our God lacks nothing.

If we look at ourselves honestly, we will admit our insufficiency and trust in our mighty God, who is able to supply all our needs. In our weakness, He gives us strength (Isaiah 40:29–31). In our fear, He calms our soul (Isaiah 41:10–13). In our emptiness and thirst, Christ fills us to overflowing (John 4:14). In our hunger, Christ, the Living Bread, satisfies us and gives us life eternal (John 6:51). In our loneliness or grief, Jesus comforts us. He lifts us up from the pit of discouragement into the joy of His presence and the security of His love. Remember, we have no need in our lives that God cannot meet. God is sufficient! If we lack, perhaps our faith is too small, too shallow. We can trust Him to give us the strength we need for any trial. Sometimes what we require is patience; it may not be the right time for God to meet that need, or He may choose to meet it in a completely unexpected way.

Let's ask God to increase and strengthen our faith. We can trust our mighty God to give us exactly what we need, just when we need it.

Dear Lord, give me a faith that will not waver or doubt, but will trust you to meet all my needs. Help me to lean upon you and put my life in your hands.
In Jesus' name, Amen.

My God is so big,
So strong and so mighty,
There's nothing my God cannot do.

—Ruth Calkin

Deep Cleaning

I surveyed my laundry room with satisfaction. The closet had been emptied, shelves wiped, and contents set in order. The windows sparkled, the appliances shone—the whole room held the freshness of having been deep-cleaned.

Hezekiah, one of Judah's kings, ordered a similar deep cleaning of the house of God. Unlike my cleaning task which took a few hours to complete, this temple cleansing took sixteen days (2 Chronicles 29:17). How much rubbish and filth Hezekiah's men must have needed to carry out! Hezekiah's idol-worshiping father had destroyed the vessels in the temple and closed the temple doors, prohibiting worship (2 Chronicles 28:24). But Hezekiah "did that which was right in the sight of the LORD" (2 Chronicles 29:2).

Because the Hebrews had forsaken God and incurred His wrath, many of them had been killed or taken into captivity. Hezekiah now urged them to humble themselves before God: "For the LORD your God is gracious and merciful, and will not turn away his face from you, if ye return unto him" (2 Chronicles 30:9). Hezekiah's people followed his urging. They destroyed the images, groves, high places, and altars used for idol worship.

Does your spiritual life need some deep cleaning? When you walk with God, the Holy Spirit faithfully nudges you, revealing areas where you have sinned or gotten sloppy about walking in truth. Repentance cleanses those spaces, and obedience sets them in order, bringing you again into clean and pure fellowship with God.

Survey the books upon your shelves,
    The things you choose to view.
Would Christ be pleased to read or watch
    These things each day with you?
Do they inspire your heart to bow
    In prayer upon your knees,
Or do they feed your fleshly lusts,
    And lure you into ease?
Be careful what you feast upon,
    The things you hear and see,
For they will claim your heart and soul—
    Determine who you'll be.

The Cost of Obedience

Hudson Taylor, founder of the China Inland Mission, surrendered his will to Christ as a young man. When he answered the call to go to China as a missionary, he had no idea how much that commitment would cost. He once wrote to his mother, "It is an easy thing to sing, 'I all on earth forsake.' It is not very difficult to think, and honestly though ignorantly to say, 'I give up all to Thee, and for Thee.' But God sometimes teaches one that that little word 'all' is terribly comprehensive."[8]

Hudson knew his call to China would separate him from family. Yet he could not foresee the tragedies ahead—watching his wife and several of his children suffer illness and death in China. He did not envision the poverty he would face or the dangers he would encounter. Yes, Hudson learned the cost of obedience, but he also learned to trust God with everything. At a conference he spoke of the path of obedience and self-denying service, remarking, "But it is in that path that God reveals Himself most."[9]

Many Bible heroes counted the cost of obedience and chose to obey God. Our greatest example is our Savior Jesus Christ, who left the riches of glory to come to earth as a man. He who had angels at His call surrendered to the will of the Father and gave His life for the whole world. His supreme sacrifice was made on our behalf. When we believe upon His name and follow Him in obedience, this brings joy to Christ.

The blessings of obedience far outweigh its cost. Are we willing to lay down our lives to obey God? It is only as we give up control of our lives that we find true life (Matthew 16:25).

Dear Lord, I have counted the cost. I surrender all, whatever that might include. Help me to obey you in the little things of life. Give me grace, Lord, to walk the path of obedience, to be faithful to you. In Jesus' name, Amen.

The cross that He gave may be heavy,

But it ne'er outweighs His grace,

The storm that I feared may surround me,

But it ne'er excludes His face.

—Ballington Booth

Instrument of Torture

We see its shape embedded in the ornate stained glass of a cathedral, or adorning the wall behind the pulpit of a multimillion dollar church building. But there was nothing pretty about the cross of Calvary. This wooden structure was an instrument of torture. It was not prepared for good people, but for the vilest of men, criminals of the basest sort. The cross represented shame. Calvary and Golgotha[e] both mean "place of skulls," a place of death. The cross, with its rough splinters, inflicted pain upon those who hung there.

When Jesus told His disciples to take up their cross and follow Him, they knew they were not facing a life of ease. This meant hardship and ridicule—perhaps beating or stoning. It meant leaving family, home, friends, and all things familiar. It might mean suffering hunger, pain, or poverty, but it also meant finding joy, peace, and eternity with Christ. Jesus' followers gladly bore their crosses, giving their all for the cause of Christ. They saw the cross as the gate to the path to heaven. Christ crucified, the Son of Glory, became the theme of their message.

For the Christian, the cross has not changed. It still means death—death to self and the old life. But it also means a new life, a new beginning. Bearing the cross costs us everything, and yet it means knowing Christ in deep, intimate way. Surrender leads to joy and peace as we

---

[e] *Calvary* comes from the Latin term and *Golgotha* from Aramaic and Greek.

humble ourselves at the feet of Jesus. To carry the cross we have to bend not only our backs, but also our knees to the lordship of Jesus Christ.

Christ's blood sacrifice made the way for us to be overcomers. He overcame sin and death so we can too. Life doesn't end at the cross, it begins. And this new life blossoms fuller and richer than the life we had known. Christ offers life abundant and full of glory, both here and in the world to come. Embrace the cross, that instrument of torture; cling to it. Allow self to be put to death. Then awake, arise to newness of life in Christ. Put on the garment of salvation, and rejoice to follow in the footsteps of Jesus.

Dear Lord, I surrender all to follow you. I will bear my cross with joy. Thank you for overcoming sin and giving me that same power. In Jesus' name, Amen.

O Cross, that liftest up my head,
I dare not ask to hide from Thee;
I lay in dust life's glory dead,
And from the ground there blossoms red
Life that shall endless be.[f]

[f] "O Love That Will Not Let Me Go," v. 4.

Denying Self

Hudson Taylor once said, "Self-denial surely means something far greater than some slight and insignificant lessening of our self-indulgences."[10] We live in an age of intemperance and self-ishness, when the primary focus for many people is looking out for number one. In stark contrast to this mentality, Jesus told His disciples, "If any man will come after me, let him deny himself, and take up his cross, and follow me" (Matthew 16:24). He also told them, "And he that taketh not his cross, and followeth after me, is not worthy of me" (Matthew 10:38). What does it mean to deny ourselves?

Jesus asks us to conform to His will. He calls us to a life of self-denial, going against our flesh, and laying down our will to follow Him. Christ's way, though sometimes hard, is the only way to God and the glory that awaits us. As L. E. Maxwell put it, "Our call to embrace the Cross is a call to reign with Christ."[11]

Jesus still bears the scars from His sufferings on the cross. When He returns, will we be wearing scars or will we have taken the easy road, shunning the cross as too heavy and harsh? Will Christ recognize us as His own?

Amy Carmichael, missionary to India, penned a poem that relates to this theme. Having given fifty-six years of her life to orphan chil-dren in India, she had suffered for Christ many times. Yet she bore her cross with joy, and her life has inspired many. May we, too, willingly lay down our selfish will and embrace the cross. Someday we'll reign with Christ!

Dear Lord, grant me strength daily to joyfully take up my cross, suffer scars and show my love for you.
In Jesus' name, Amen.

Hast thou no scar?
No hidden scar on foot, or side, or hand?
I hear thee sung as mighty in the land,
I hear them hail thy bright ascendant star,
Hast thou no scar?

Hast thou no wound?
Yet I was wounded by the archers, spent,
Leaned me against a tree to die; and rent
By ravening beasts that compassed me, I swooned:
Hast thou no wound?

No wound? No scar?
Yet, as the Master shall the servant be,
And pierced are the feet that follow Me;
But thine are whole; can he have followed far
Who has no wound nor scar?

—Amy Carmichael

Jars of Clay

"But we have this treasure in earthen vessels, that the excellency of the power may be of God, and not of us" (2 Corinthians 4:7). What a wonder that the divine life of Christ indwells us clay pots, these dust-formed humans! Do we realize the glorious treasure we contain, we who believe in Jesus Christ? The divine Light of the Gospel dwells within us. Thus any good we accomplish does not result from our power, but from God's. Our aim should be that others would see Christ and His greatness and power, not us.

Today's reading exhorts us to be "a vessel unto honour, sanctified, and meet for the master's use, and prepared unto every good work" (2 Timothy 2:21). That is our purpose, to be used by the Master to fulfill His plan, not our own. Paul gives a warning in Romans to those who question God: "Shall the thing formed say to him that formed it, 'Why hast thou made me thus?' Hath not the potter power over the clay . . .?" (Romans 9:20–21). Just as we have no right to claim the credit for the wonderful plan being lived out in us, neither can we complain about the way the Master made us or how He chooses to use us.

We are simple jars of clay. Without Christ within us shining His light, our lives have little worth; with Christ in us, we bring Him glory. Pascal wrote, "Do small things as if they were great, because of the majesty of Jesus Christ, who works them in us, and who lives our life; and great things as small and easy, because of His omnipotence."[12]

Charles Fox called the following list God's five-ranked army of decreasing human weakness. It is those who are:

FOOLISH enough to depend on Him for wisdom;

WEAK enough to be empowered with His strength;

BASE enough to have no honor, but God's honor;

DESPISED enough to be kept in the dust at His feet;

NOTHING enough for God to be everything.[13]

Without Christ's supreme sacrifice for us upon the cross, we would never have experienced the wonder of His presence, the joy of forgiveness, and the power of His life within us. We have nothing of which to boast, but Christ must receive all glory, honor, and praise.

Dear Lord, keep before me the knowledge that I am but a vessel for your honor. May I exalt your name in all I do. In Jesus' name, Amen.

Not I, but Christ, be honored, loved, exalted;

Not I, but Christ, be seen, be known, be heard;

Not I, but Christ, in every look and action;

Not I, but Christ, in every thought and word.

—Ada A. Whiddington

Scripture reading: 2 Thessalonians 1:1–12

Counted Worthy

*T*ribulations. Persecutions. As the church in Thessalonica felt the heat of the refiner's fire, the Apostle Paul prayed that they would be counted worthy of the kingdom of God. Today in many parts of the world, Christians still face persecution. We shudder when we read of the anger and hatred directed toward them and the atrocities inflicted upon them because of their faith in Jesus Christ. Christians in America are just beginning to feel the pressure of those who mock Christianity.

Little by little, Satan has been gaining ground in religious circles as many churches forsake the teachings of God's Word. More and more, the boundaries God set are being pushed aside to allow "freedom" to do whatever one wishes.

As evil escalates in this world, we can expect more persecution. Are we prepared to stand for Christ whatever the cost? Does our loyalty to Him outweigh our fear of man? We need not fear the future, for the Holy Spirit will comfort and encourage in that day so we can be faithful to Christ.

When the darkness of sin presses in around us, look up! As Paul says in 2 Thessalonians 2:16–17, God and Jesus Himself have given us "everlasting consolation and good hope" and are ready to comfort us and establish us in our work. What a security to know we are supported by a God who will never be defeated!

Are we prepared to stand for Christ when trials come? Do we know where to turn for comfort and support? Take courage, dear friend. Look up! Our Lord is coming soon! May He find us worthy.

Dear Lord, help me to keep close to you, so I can be true to you whatever comes. Thank you for redeeming me and counting me worthy to suffer this trial for your kingdom. In Jesus' name, Amen.

If our land should be o'ertaken
    And our freedom be no more,
If they say you must forsake Him
    Who your sins and burdens bore,
Will you listen to their threat'nings,
    Or with firm conviction vow,
"Though it cost me pain and suff'ring,
    I will stand for Jesus now!"

This Moment of Time

"What time is it?"
    "How much time will it take?"
"It's time to go!"

Time. How much it matters to us! We all have the same amount, yet we always wish for more. We feel like we don't have enough of it to accomplish all we need or would like to do. Do we have too many claims on our time, or do we fail to use our minutes wisely?

Time—the indefinite, continued progress of existence. No matter our stage in life, we have a past, a present, and a future. Some have only a few short years. Others live a century or more.

We cannot stop time's relentless march or peer into the future. We have only this moment to live. You may think, *What can I do with just one moment of time? What is it worth?* Time is precious because it is fleeting. We never know when our time may be up, and our soul will leave the body.

Uncertainties fill our lives, and evil abounds in our world. Because of this, we must seize every opportunity to invest our time for the Lord. We must search His word daily, so we can align our lives to its lessons, keeping our hearts and lives pure. We also need to reach out to others, sharing the message of Jesus Christ with them. Our time belongs not to us, but to Christ. We can selfishly horde our time for ourselves, but we will find no lasting pleasure or satisfaction—only emptiness and restless craving for more. When we use our time to honor and glorify God, inner peace assures us we have done the right thing.

The devil wants to keep you too busy to think. Take time today to consider what you are doing with your moments. The seconds, minutes, hours, days, and years pass by so quickly. One moment you possess the freshness of youth. The next, you feel the sunset of the golden years. Seek God's will, and use your moments to serve Him. Remember, what you do with this moment of time determines where your soul will spend eternity.

> *Dear Lord, I want to give you all my moments, my days, my life. Help me to work for your kingdom, to redeem the time. I want a willing heart to do your will.*
> *In Jesus' name, Amen.*

Father, I know that all my life
    Is portioned out for me;
The changes that are sure to come,
    I do not fear to see:
I ask Thee for a present mind,
    Intent on pleasing Thee.

In service which Thy will appoints
    There are no bonds for me;
My inmost heart is taught the truth
    That makes Thy children free;
A life of self–renouncing love
    Is one of liberty.

—Anna L. Waring

"I Am Persuaded"

Cancer! That dreaded word. Two years ago when I was diagnosed with a rare form of cancer, I wondered, "What does my future hold?" I remembered the Apostle Paul's strong assurance that nothing can separate us from the love of God. As we often do when we face misfortunes, such as illness, death, or loss of possessions, I thought of Romans 8:28: "And we know that all things work together for good to them that love God, to them who are the called according to his purpose." When difficulty or tragedy strikes, it does not mean God does not love us. However, our response to these things may prove whether or not we love and trust Him.

When life goes smoothly, we may imagine we're in charge. Then we hit a rough spot and are reminded that our life is not our own, but God's. He gave us life, and He can take it. Can we accept His plan and purpose for our life even though we don't understand it? He knows our reluctance to face adversities, afflictions, and infirmities. In all these things, though, remember—not even death can separate us from the love of God.

The eye of faith sees beyond the death of this fleshly body. Through the power of Christ's resurrection, we can know the joy of an endless life in the presence of our Savior. We are conquerors through Him who loves us (Romans 8:37). When our hope rests on Jesus, we are never abandoned. God's love enfolds us.

We can say with Paul, "For I am persuaded, that neither death, nor life, nor angels, nor principalities, nor powers, nor things present, nor things to come, nor height, nor depth, nor any other creature, shall be able to separate us from the love of God, which is in Christ Jesus our Lord" (Romans 8:38–39). We can face the uncertainties ahead without fear; God loves and cares for us.

> *Dear heavenly Father, thank you for your unfailing love surrounding and upholding us as we trust in Christ.*
> *In Jesus' name, Amen.*

Not all that men on earth can do,
Nor powers high nor low,
Shall cause His mercy to remove,
Or wrest us from His love.[g]

—Isaac Watts

[g] "Who Shall the Lord's Elect Condemn?"
The Christian Hymnary, #650, v.4.

Procrastination

I'll do it later.

How often do we put off what we know we should do? Maybe it takes too much effort to discipline the children when they quarrel or too much energy to rise early to have devotions before the family awakes. But procrastination only causes regret.

In the story of the ten virgins, all had burning lamps, but only five had extra oil in case the bridegroom came later than they anticipated (Matthew 25:1–13). The other five put off going for more oil. Perhaps they thought, "He will come soon, and our oil will last until then." But when his arrival was announced, the foolish virgins saw that their lamps had drawn up the last drops of oil. As they hurried off to buy more, the bridegroom came. Only the wise virgins, whose lamps were burning, accompanied him to the feast. The foolish, made tardy by their short-sightedness, were turned away.

Procrastination costs dearly. Yet it comes so naturally! Have we heard the Word, seen a need in our lives, but gone on without doing anything about it? Have we soothed our consciences by thinking we will have time for it later? Or maybe we think it doesn't really matter. Let us heed Christ's warning, "Watch therefore, for ye know neither the day nor the hour wherein the Son of man cometh" (Matthew 25:13). As Stephen Grellet put it, "I shall pass through this world but once. Any good therefore that I can do or any kindness that I can show to any human being, let me do it now. Let me not defer or neglect it, for I shall not pass this way again."[14]

Christ's coming will surprise those who aren't watching. He will return without warning, startling the unwatchful out of their sleepy apathy. We must be ready at all times! We must daily keep our lives in order, obeying God's Word wholeheartedly. How sad to be caught unaware because we put off doing what God has said to do!

Dear Lord, I don't want to procrastinate. I want be ready at all times for your coming. In Jesus' name, Amen.

When Jesus comes to reward His servants,
    Whether it be noon or night,
Faithful to Him will He find us watching,
    With our lamps all trimmed and bright?
Oh, can we say we are ready, brother?
    Ready for the soul's bright home?
Say, will He find you and me still watching,
    Waiting, waiting when the Lord shall come?

—Fanny Crosby[h]

[h] "Will Jesus Find Us Watching?" *Christian Hymnal,* #284.

Watch and Pray

What is that smell? A scorched odor wafted through the cold air to where my son was stacking wood. Suddenly he remembered. He had been boiling down sap from his maple trees, and had forgotten to watch the syrup. Ruefully he surveyed the dark caramelized layer in the pan. For want of careful tending, the syrup had been ruined.

Our souls also need careful watching. Satan tries to trip us, bringing temptation into our path. But watching is not enough by itself. We can see a temptation approaching, but without prayer, we lack the backbone to turn from it.

In the account in Mark 14, Jesus told Peter, James, and John to watch and pray while He went aside to pray in solitude. Christ agonized in prayer, sweating what appeared to be large drops of blood (Luke 22:44). Each time He returned to the disciples, He found them sleeping. Jesus faced that hour alone, but He won the battle. He surrendered His will to the Father, ready to lay down His life so we could live.

Later that night, a fearful Peter denied Christ three times. Would he have responded differently if he had prayed with his Master when he was asked?

Earlier in His ministry, Jesus had spoken to His disciples of the coming end times, warning them to watch and pray (Mark 13:33). None but the Father knows when Christ will return (Mark 13:32).

On that great day, no longer will we have time or opportunity to make things right. Christians will rejoice, but unbelievers will tremble. What we have done with our opportunities will determine our response to the coming of that day.

Let us heed Paul's admonition: "Watch ye, stand fast in the faith, quit you like men, be strong" (1 Corinthians 16:13). Sisters, let us watch and pray. It is vital to the health of our souls.

Dear Lord, give me strength to be faithful to you and to be more diligent in praying for the unsaved. I want to be ready when you return. In Jesus' name, Amen.

O watch and pray! In faith be strong,
    Be listening for His call.
Let not your heart be turned aside;
    Through faith, you will not fall.

At Midnight

My mother used to say if young people stay out later than midnight, it only leads to trouble. Jesus said men loved darkness rather than light because their deeds were evil (John 3:19). Satan thought darkness and death had triumphed when Christ died. Darkness has been the breeding place of wickedness for a long time, but praise the Lord, Christ overcame the darkness. He defeated evil once and for all—He arose!

In the parable of the ten virgins, only five were prepared for that midnight cry, "The bridegroom comes!" (Matthew 25:6). Presumably when Christ returns, many clocks around the world will not show midnight, but He will come at an hour when many are not expecting Him. Midnight arrives with intense darkness. As spiritual darkness increases in the world, we must be watching and waiting for the "midnight hour" when Christ will return.

Each of us will face our "midnight," the time when our bodies cease to function and we take our last breath. Are we ready for that time? Have we used our time wisely?

When Paul and Silas were jailed for preaching the Gospel, midnight found them singing and praying to God (Acts 16:25–33). God honored their faith by sending an earthquake to open the prison doors and release their chains. The jailor, certain that the prisoners had all escaped, was about to commit suicide when Paul assured him all were there. Sensing these were men of God, the jailer asked Paul, "What must I do to be saved?" A miraculous earthquake at midnight had brought this man to repentance. Good things can happen at midnight, too.

As Christians, our hope soars beyond this life. Midnight will blaze into glorious dawn when Jesus comes to claim His own, ushering in a glorious everlasting day. Be ready!

Dear Lord, I want to be ready for your return, no matter what the time. In Jesus' name, Amen.

It may be at morn, when the day is awaking,
When sunlight through darkness and shadow is breaking,
That Jesus will come in the fullness of glory,
To receive from the world His own.

It may be at midday, it may be at twilight,
It may be, perchance, that the blackness of midnight
Will burst into light in the blaze of His glory,
When Jesus receives His own.

—H. L. Turner

Nothing Between

"Look at all these weeds!" I exclaimed. "These vines are going to take over our walk. Let's pull them out, children."

As we pulled, I thought of the chorus of an old song. "Nothing between my soul and the Savior, / So that His blessed face may be seen; / Nothing preventing the least of His favor; / Keep the way clear! Let nothing between."[i] How important to keep the path between us open and free of obstacles.

Romans 8:38–39 tells us that nothing can separate us from the love of God. Nothing can—unless we allow it to. Like the weeds we pulled, pesky sin habits can sprout in our hearts, sown by Satan. Perhaps the sin of neglect takes root. Satan whispers, "You don't have time to read the Bible this morning. You can do it later." If we listen to him, soon those weeds of neglect will begin to choke our communication pathway to God.

Perhaps you have heard the statement, "Grass doesn't grow on the path between friends." Friends use the pathway of communication often. If we neglect to pray and read the Bible, weeds such as envy, bitterness, self-will, pride, and anger will fill the path between us and God.

Has something come between you and the Savior? Even legitimate

[i] C.A. Tindley, "Nothing Between."

things can crowd in between us and God. We can become too busy doing good things, and not have time for the best. Hebrews 4:16 tells us to "come boldly to the throne of grace, that we may obtain mercy, and find grace to help in time of need." How gracious is our heavenly Father to forgive us and clear the pathway between us.

Nothing matters more than your relationship with the Lord. If you would be with Him forever, you must stay close to Him now. May your feet wear smooth the path leading to the mercy seat.

> *Dear Lord, help me to keep a close relationship with you.*
> *Thank you for your mercy and love. I can't wait to see you!*
> *In Jesus' name, Amen.*

I would keep clear the cherished path
    Between God's heart and mine,
So I can run without delay
    For strength which is divine.

I would not have one thing to mar
    The fellowship we know,
So daily I will bow in prayer;
    Allow no weeds to grow.

Scripture reading: Genesis 2:18–25

God's Plan for You

Haven't we all heard men say, "I'll never understand women"? Sometimes we feel no one understands us. No one knows what we need or brings us fulfillment. If we're looking to anyone or anything besides Jesus Christ to meet all our needs, we will be disappointed.

But God made woman. Our Creator totally understands us. He knows our needs—physical, mental, emotional, and above all, spiritual. Without a relationship with God through Christ, we will feel empty, helpless, and unfulfilled, in spite of any feigned independence.

From the beginning God had a plan. He wanted a group of people on this beautiful earth with whom He could fellowship. After God created Adam, He made Eve using one of Adam's ribs. Now Adam had someone to love who would also love him. God, the Author of love, understands our need for love and acceptance.

Not every woman becomes a wife, but we all can be part of God's family. As His daughters, we find fulfillment, contentment, and joy. Remember, God planned it that way. God does not class women as second-rate people, unworthy of His notice. As Elisabeth Elliot put it, "The fact that I am a woman does not make me a different kind of Christian, but the fact that I am a Christian makes me a different kind of woman."[15]

Open your heart to God, asking Him to show you how much He

loves and values you. Allow God's Word to speak to you, and feel His presence surrounding you. Become a woman who glorifies her Lord and Savior. Jesus will meet your every need.

Dear Lord, thank you for making me your daughter. Help me to please and to glorify you every day. I want to love you always. In Jesus' name, Amen.

Created for a purpose—
    The Lord has plans for you;
So look unto your Father;
    What would He have you do?

You'll find joy and contentment
    In following His plan,
And knowing that He loves you.
    He holds you in His hand.

A Virtuous Woman

"Who can find a virtuous woman?" (Proverbs 31:10). A woman of high principle, who is honest, chaste, just, and uncorrupted by this world. Scripture says her worth exceeds precious gems. In today's world of loose morals, a woman of virtue stands out. Few brides or grooms enter into marriage as virgins. Oh sisters, are we raising our daughters as virtuous women? Are we setting a worthy example for others to follow?

The virtuous woman does her husband good all the days of her life (Proverbs 31:12). Do we make this our goal? We naturally tend to think of ourselves first, but honoring the authorities God has placed over us will bring a blessing.

Doing good involves our finances. The wise woman of Proverbs 31 employs her hands with diligence. She gardens, shops for food, and sews for her family. She reaches out to the poor and needy. As the community sees her kindness and generosity, her husband's status soars. Everyone recognizes he truly has a good wife.

The Proverbs 31 woman enjoys a great deal of liberty. Her husband knows he can trust her to make wise decisions, as together they live out their shared sense of purpose. She practices thrift, using her resources wisely so she has more to give. Even those with a limited income can find ways to help others.

Your actions as a wife reflect upon your husband. Are you doing good to him if you waste money on unnecessary items? Perhaps you begrudge the hours your husband spends working, wishing he could spend more time at home. But careless spending may mean he must work long hours to make ends meet.

Remember, sisters, as you honor your husband, you also honor God. As you practice doing good to your husband, your marriage will flourish, and your love will grow.

Dear Lord, thank you for my husband. Help me to honor him, and do good to him all the days of my life. I praise you for giving me someone who loves and cares for me. In Jesus' name, Amen.

Women of God can never be like women of the world.
The world has enough women who are tough;
  We need women who are tender.
There are enough women who are coarse;
  We need women who are kind.
There are enough women who are rude;
  We need women who are refined.
We have enough women of fame and fortune;
  We need more women of faith.
We have enough greed; we need more goodness.
  We have enough vanity; we need more virtue.
We have enough popularity; we need more purity.[16]

—Margaret Nadauld

Evidence of Transformation

Kevin[j] and his young family had been attending our church for a while. One Sunday morning, he surrendered to Christ. When my husband and I visited him later, he would often be reading his Bible—and smoking a cigarette. He said, "I'm trying, but I can't seem to quit smoking." One day we prayed with Kevin and encouraged him to ask God for deliverance. That prayer was answered, and our friend never smoked again.

Kevin's life bore even more evidence of the transforming power of Jesus. For many years he had stolen tools from the factory where he worked. After his conversion, he went to the factory president and confessed his theft. He compiled a list of all the stolen goods he could recall and offered to pay whatever his employer deemed fair.

Kevin's employer listened, stunned—not that his employee had stolen, but that he had confessed and wanted to make restitution. He forgave Kevin and refused to accept any payment for the stolen items. Kevin told his boss he had confessed because he had become a Christian, and he believed Jesus wanted him to make things right. His transformed life witnessed powerfully to his employer.

Christ wants to set us free, change our desires, give us hope, and fill us with His peace and joy. In Romans 12:2 we read, "And be not

[j] Not his real name.

conformed to this world: but be ye transformed by the renewing of your mind, that ye may prove what is that good, and acceptable, and perfect, will of God." Does your life manifest the fruits of transformation?

Dear Lord, thank you for changing me and giving me a desire to follow and please you. In Jesus' name, Amen.

Like the ocean gently swelling,
    As its breakers crest and fall,
So the love of Jesus calls us;
    "Will you come?" O heed His call.

As our souls He gently washes
    In the blood He shed for us,
We can feel the joy within us
    Surging up in waves of trust.

What a change takes place within us!
    Transformation Christ has wrought,
Making us a new creation;
    Praise the Lord! Our souls He bought.

What Family Do You Resemble?

"Are you a Webb?" A stranger approached my son and asked him the question. The woman thought my son looked like the father of some children she had cared for. The father she was thinking of happened to be my son's second cousin. Shared traits identify us as members of a particular family.

As Christians we also belong to a family—the family of God. Can others quickly pick us out as members of that family? Do they say, "She must be a Christian; she has the characteristics of that family"? Galatians 5:22–23 lists the qualities of a child of God, the fruit of the Spirit. These fruits show that we belong to the family of God.

Love comes first on the list. Jesus says, "By this shall all men know that ye are my disciples, if ye have love one to another" (John 13:35). This identifies us to all around us.

Peace follows. Colossians 3:13–15 commands us to forgive others as Christ has forgiven us, to love, and to allow the peace of God to govern our hearts. The family of God shares this characteristic.

"Patience and longsuffering with joyfulness," further identify us as members of God's family (Colossians 1:11). James 3:17 describes the kind of wisdom God's family shares: "pure, then peaceable, gentle, and easy to be intreated, full of mercy and good fruits, without partiality, and without hypocrisy."

Today's reading provides an additional list of qualities to emulate: faith, virtue (which includes morality, integrity, and goodness), knowledge, temperance, patience, godliness, brotherly kindness, and charity (2 Peter 1:5–7).

Can the world clearly see whose family we are part of? Are people attracted to the Jesus they see in us?

Dear Lord, help me to portray you in the way I live each day. May others be able to see you and desire to also be part of your family. In Jesus' name, Amen.

More like the Master I would ever be,

More of His meekness, more humility;

More zeal to labor, more courage to be true,

More consecration for work He bids me do.

—Charles Gabriel

Reality of Marriage

A little house with a white picket fence, a devoted husband, chubby-cheeked children . . . Did your dreams for the future look something like this? Why does marriage sometimes fall short of your dreams? Why do our closest relationships sometimes disappoint us?

Consider, first of all, your relationship with God. Do you live out His priorities? If you crave a deeper walk with God, learn to know Him better through reading His Word and prayer. Examine your heart; have you yielded to His will? Do you listen to His Spirit? These are the secrets to successful relationships.

Although today's Scripture reading does not specifically mention marriage, it speaks to the heart of the matter: "And thou shalt love the LORD thy God with all thine heart, and with all thy soul, and with all thy might" (Deuteronomy 6:5). The more we love God, the more He enables us to love others. Those who allow God to meet their deepest emotional needs are best prepared to give themselves in marriage.

Think back to the way you related to your father. Did you respect him and submit to his authority? Did you appreciate his correction and the limits he set? Learning to trust your father's decisions prepared you to relate to your husband. If you struggled to submit to your father, that may be how you respond to your husband's leadership.

A strong marriage requires more than mutual attraction. It takes mutual dependence upon and commitment to God. Marriage brings struggles when one or both partners have failed to stay close to God. Outside influences can bring stressful situations, but our responses depend upon our closeness to the Father.

Remembering our first year of marriage, I marvel at our youth and immaturity—two eighteen-year-olds with little teaching about courtship or marriage. But what we did have was a solid commitment to God. This, and our firm belief in the sanctity and permanence of marriage, helped us through those early adjustments.

Never be too proud to admit you need help in your spiritual life or in your marriage. Realize that you can't change the person you marry; only God can do that. Instead, pray, "God, change me. Help me to be more loving, kind, and respectful." If problems arise in your marriage, don't blame your spouse—look for ways you can improve. There is no room for self in a marriage if it is to be a happy one.

Dear sister, devote yourself to serving Christ with all your heart, soul, and mind. Whether married or not, you will find blessing beyond measure as you abide in His will.

> *Dear Lord, help me to draw closer to you, putting you first in my life, and seeking your will in all things. In Jesus' name, Amen.*

Lord, give us Christian homes!
Homes where the Bible is loved and taught,
Homes where the Master's will is sought,
Homes crowned with beauty Thy love hath wrought;
Lord, give us Christian homes!

—B. B. McKinney

The Sanctity of Marriage

God officiated in the very first wedding. He ordained marriage as a permanent bond between one man and one woman. Jesus says, "For this cause shall a man leave his father and his mother, and shall cleave unto his wife; and they twain shall be one flesh" (Mark 10:7–8). Cleave means to stick, cling, or be glued together.

Society's attempt to redefine marriage, blatantly disregarding that which God established, has brought marriage into a vulnerable position. The institution of marriage ought to be impregnable—a fortified position that cannot be taken by force, a stronghold resistant to attack or criticism. God wants our marriages to be strong, like a city enclosed and fortified. We know, however, Satan tries to destroy what God has planned. As people fall away from God, their marriages and homes disintegrate.

What can we do as Christian women to preserve and strengthen our marriages? Our relationship with Christ is our first priority. If our love for God grows cold, we open ourselves to moral impurity and marital infidelity.

Never entertain the thought of dissolving your marriage, for Jesus says, "What therefore God hath joined together, let not man put asunder" (Mark 10:9). If you feel a distance between you and your husband, beware! When others are choosing their own way regardless of whom it affects, may we hold marriage sacred and do all we can to preserve and enhance our marriage. Children grow up hurting and insecure because of the breakdown of homes. Pray for strength against the enemy of our souls, who wants to destroy God's plan for marriage. May God be our strong defense!

Dear Lord, by your grace I want to help build a strong marriage that will stand for a lifetime. Help me to stay close to you. In Jesus' name, Amen.

Our God designed the marriage bond
    To hold 'til death does part.
God calls the man to be the head,
    The wife to share his heart.

Respect and honor she should give,
    He is to love her more—
His love portrays the love of Christ,
    And both the Lord adore.

Love That Endures

The bride and groom had eyes only for each other. Their faces glowed, and their hands were clasped. Then just a few years later, we heard they were getting a divorce. What happened to all their glowing emotions?

A good marriage needs a solid foundation. When couples leave God out of their marriage, they build on unstable ground. When storms come, the foundation erodes.

God intends marriage to portray Christ and His bride, the church. A strong, godly marriage preaches the Gospel in a powerful way. Satan knows this, and does all he can to destroy unity. Christ, out of love, gave everything—position, comfort, His very life—to redeem His bride. Similarly, enduring marriages cannot be built without sacrificial love. When both husband and wife put Christ first, the fires of difficulty will only purify and strengthen their love.

Picture your marriage as yourself and your husband climbing the two sides of a step ladder. The higher both of you climb toward Christ, resembling Him more, the closer you come together. When you seek the best interests of your husband, you will never use affection to gain what you want, but delight in pleasing him.

Our actions reveal whether we really mean the words of love we say, as the Apostle John urges, "My little children, let us not love in word, neither in tongue; but in deed and in truth" (1 John 3:18). What do your actions show?

Dear Lord, help me to love sacrificially. I want my marriage to be built upon you so that our love will endure. In Jesus' name, Amen.

Marriage Takes Three

I once thought marriage took,
    Just two to make a go.
But now I'm convinced,
    It takes the Lord also.

And not one marriage fails,
    Where Christ is asked to enter.
As lovers come together,
    With Jesus at the center.

In homes where Christ is first,
    It's obvious to see.
Those unions really work,
    For marriage still takes three.[17]

—Jasmine Cruz

Finding Our All in Christ

I once met a woman who had had two abusive husbands. She raised her children alone while holding down a job. Sadly, she keeps looking for the perfect man who will meet her needs.

Only God can satisfy the soul. Trying to fill that God-shaped void within them, some people give themselves to other "lovers" such as achievement, wealth, alcohol, or drugs. These pursuits do nothing to quell their feelings of insecurity or despair. Others fear being alone, afraid to face the reality of who they are or what they have done, so they seek distraction and fulfillment in unhealthy ways. Some go the opposite way and decide they don't need anyone. They defiantly declare their independence, believing they can control their own lives and answer to no one.

We are created with a need for companionship. Our Father placed that inside our hearts intending it to enrich our lives. He wants us to enjoy each other socially, but no matter how many friendships we have, none compares with the fellowship we experience with God. As we give ourselves completely to Him, we will find deep, satisfying intimacy. He meets our needs, understands us perfectly, and fills our lonely hearts.

The woman who conversed with Jesus at the well in today's reading felt an aching void. Relational chaos defined her history—a succession of five husbands, followed by her current live-in. Jesus offered her living water, but He also exposed her sin. Jesus still offers the water of life, but to receive it we must face ourselves as sinners in need of Jesus.

Jesus asks us to give up our independence and lean on Him. He loves you already and waits for you to respond to His call. He pursues your heart. Will you yield to His embrace?

> *Dear Lord, thank you for calling me to come and drink your living water! I can depend on you in every situation. Thank you for being my all in all. In Jesus' name, Amen.*

O Christ our All in each, our All in all!
Others have this or that, a love, a friend,
A trusted teacher, a long worked for end:
But what to me were Peter or were Paul
Without Thee? fame or friend if such might be?
Thee wholly will I love, Thee wholly seek,
Follow Thy foot-track, hearken for Thy call.
O Christ mine All in all, my flesh is weak,
A trembling fawning tyrant unto me:
Turn, look upon me, let me hear Thee speak:
Tho' bitter billows of Thine utmost sea
Swathe me, and darkness build around its wall,
Yet will I rise, Thou lifting when I fall,
And if Thou hold me fast, yet cleave to Thee.[18]

—Christina Georgina Rossetti

Maintaining Moral Purity

As a young married woman with no children, I worked as a nurse aide in a hospital. One morning as we stood around the desk waiting for reports, a middle-aged doctor walked up beside me and slid his arm around my shoulders. I had seen him do this to others, even hugging them tightly or caressing them.

Immediately I stepped away, putting distance between us. Later I heard a nurse tell him, "You won't get that one. She's a Christian." He laughed, but he never attempted anything again. What if I had tolerated his advances? No doubt it would have tarnished my co-workers' view of Christianity and of my sincerity.

Working with the opposite gender often fosters a dangerous familiarity. Seeds of impurity—an impure thought, a lustful look, a forbidden touch—take root and grow if provided fertile soil. Only by God's help can we remain pure in this decaying world. Through prayer we find the power to keep our minds pure and the wisdom to avoid situations that might lead to temptation. God offers us strength to look the other way, turn aside, and think of Christ instead. Having close accountability with a respected fellow believer is a powerful tool in helping us remain free from such situations.

With society sliding towards permissiveness of evil, how can we help our children value moral purity? We must explain to them the snare of immoral thoughts, which often lead to immoral deeds. We must urge them to keep themselves pure so they will have no regrets.

Let us watch over what our children read, and with whom they associate regularly. We should know where they are going and with whom. Most of all, we must teach them to fear God. God loves them, and He will help them to live in purity. He protects His children!

Dear Lord, help me to maintain moral purity and to teach my children to look to you for help when temptations come. Thank you for loving us and preparing a way of escape as we call upon you. In Jesus' name, Amen.

Lord, we want to keep our hearts
    Holy, pure, and true.
Help us to keep our eyes and minds
    Focused, Lord, on you.

Impelling Love

"*I* just love this handbag!"

"I love coffee and chocolate!"

How often we hear the word *love* used casually! We may use the word to refer to different kinds of attachments, and different degrees of intensity, but true love springs only from God. The ultimate Lover, He has shown the greatest degree of love ever known. Love moved Him to send His only Son Jesus to earth to die for us (John 3:16). Jesus exemplifies real love, a love that impelled Him to action. For three years on earth, His love reached out to heal the sick, care for the poor and neglected, and offer hope to those who would believe. When at the cross He laid down His life for the world, His sacrifice of love and obedience pleased God.

When we love our husbands, we don't find it a hardship to serve them, to submit to them, or do the things that please them. Our love impels us to go beyond mere duty. Similarly, our love for Christ should move us to put Him first in our lives. It moves us to consider His instructions, His examples and desires before our own. We should aim to live solely to please the Lord.

Does gratitude for our deliverance impel us to lavish our Deliverer with grateful, loving service? Christ desires us to walk in love and obedience, offering our devotion to Him. He does not want empty words or meaningless promises. If we love Him, we will show our love with action.

Dear Lord, thank you for loving me to such a great extent. I want to love you with a fervency that impels me to action. In Jesus' name, Amen.

And can it be that I should gain
An interest in the Savior's blood?
Died He for me, who caused His pain?
For me, who Him to death pursued?

Amazing love! how can it be
That thou, my God, should die for me!

He left His Father's throne above,
So free, so infinite His grace;
Emptied Himself of all but love,
And bled for Adam's helpless race;
'Tis mercy all, immense and free;
For, O my God, it found out me.

Amazing love! how can it be
That thou, my God, should die for me!

—Charles Wesley

A Wise Woman

Do you ever feel like a gerbil on a wheel, churning through a ceaseless round of meal preparation, dirty dishes, cleaning tasks, and piles of laundry? Sometimes the daily grind overwhelms us. Take heart, dear sisters. Your labors may go unnoticed by others, but you serve a God who prizes humble faithfulness—even cups of water given in His name. A wise woman will focus on the important things: loving God and your family.

Consider the Proverbs 31 woman who "openeth her mouth with wisdom; and in her tongue is the law of kindness" (v. 26). When your children are grown, they will remember if you yelled at them or if you spoke gently. The times you prayed with them will stick in their minds longer than the times of discipline. Yes, they need your discipline, but your loving prayers motivate them to do better. Be a woman of kindness.

Involve your children in household chores, teaching by example. A household will not run smoothly while the homemaker sits idle. "Work, then play" is a time-honored motto that has been proven wise by many. Working together bonds a family. Our children have good memories of the times we sat around the table, snapping green beans.

A wise woman loves and respects her husband. Her children, shaped by her example, rise up and call her blessed (Proverbs 31:28). Her husband does likewise.

Our outward beauty will fade with the passing years, but if we fix our gaze on our Savior, our inward beauty will flourish. People will remember our love for God and others.

Proverbs 16:16 tells us, "How much better is it to get wisdom than gold! and to get understanding rather to be chosen than silver!" Are we pursuing the things God values? Do we seek His approval instead of looking to those around us? Are we teaching our daughters to cultivate true beauty? A wise woman finds fulfillment in receiving and sharing the love of Christ.

Dear Lord, help me to be a woman of wisdom who heeds your Word and points my family and others to you. In Jesus' name, Amen.

Lord, give us Christian homes!
Homes where the mother, in queenly quest,
Strives to show others Thy way is best.
Homes where the Lord is an honored guest;
Lord, give us Christian homes!

—B. B. McKinney

Beams of Light

Tornado sirens blared in the night! We made our way down the basement steps without delay. Soon the light blinked off, so we sat in total darkness, trying to save the batteries in our small flashlights. When the danger had passed, we shone the flashlight beams on the stairs so we wouldn't stumble as we climbed. How grateful we felt for those little beams of light!

As we make our way through this life, we will surely stumble without Christ, the Light of life, to guide us. In Him we find life and light rather than the death and darkness we deserve. Jesus came to shine His beacon light of truth in this sin-ravaged world. Though some believed in Christ, most turned their backs to His beam. Though they crucified Him, darkness could not snuff out His light. He rose again, shining forth like dawn.

We live in this glorious dawn, awash with His light and truth when we awake to faith in Christ. "The path of the just is as the shining light, that shineth more and more unto the perfect day" (Proverbs 4:18).

The Light reveals our inner man. Our lives should display the goodness, righteousness, and truth that please God (Ephesians 5:9–10). As we read the Bible, do we align ourselves with its truth? In the midst of our thoughts about a situation, do we ask God to shine truth on our way of thinking?

Walking in the Light also means we will with humbleness break fellowship with those who turn away to walk in darkness, warning them of their danger if they continue in that way. As Paul says in 2 Timothy 2: 24–26, we long for them to acknowledge the light of truth and recover themselves out of the snare of the devil.

Jesus says, "I am the light of the world: he that followeth me shall not walk in darkness, but shall have the light of life" (John 8:12). When we come to the Light, our walk changes. We don't want to live in sin any longer, for we see it only brings death. We give our hearts to that which has eternal value (Colossians 3:1–2).

Is your heart open to the Sonlight? Jesus is calling you to walk in His truth and find eternal joy.

Dear Lord Jesus, thank you for being that Light of life and for changing my night to day. Help me to see myself as I truly am and to worship you for who you are.
In Jesus' name, Amen.

O walk in the Light,
   The darkness shun;
Christ's way will lead home
   When life is done.

Walk Circumspectly

On an outing with my family when I was a teenager, we came upon a swinging bridge. I looked at the shaky structure, suspended above a flowing river. I noted the slack ropes that served in lieu of handrails. Before my dad allowed us to cross, he checked it thoroughly. Though I knew I could trust my dad, I still walked warily, holding onto the ropes on either side. Slowly I made my way across the swaying bridge.

My exuberant older brother bounded across the bridge, laughing merrily. "You're too cautious," he told me, but I preferred caution over getting wet. I appreciated my dad walking close to me; I knew he would keep me from falling.

God promises, "I will instruct thee and teach thee in the way which thou shalt go: I will guide thee with mine eye" (Psalm 32:8). Aren't we glad we don't have to face uncertain situations on our own? God will guide us with His perfect wisdom. Jesus has walked this way before, and His eye is upon us.

Why then do we need to walk cautiously or carefully? In our humanity, we tend to take our eyes off the Master. Then we stray from God's way or blunder into the pits Satan has dug. We also need to guard against those who try to turn us from God's way.

Only one way leads to eternal life and a heavenly home. Jesus says, "I am the way, the truth, and the life: no man cometh unto the Father, but by me" (John 14:6). Stay on track by reading, studying, and pondering God's Word. Sing psalms, hymns, and spiritual songs alone and with others.

Do not grow weary, dear sisters, but walk circumspectly— looking around and on guard against danger. Follow the trustworthy Guide. His way is perfect (Psalm 18:30).

Dear Lord, I put my faith and trust in you. I want to follow you, for I know you will lead me safely through life. In Jesus' name, Amen.

The road ahead I do not know,
   The twists and turns it makes,
But this I know—the Savior leads;
   His path is safe to take.

A Beautiful Bride

*P*icture the loveliest bride you've ever seen. What makes her stand out in comparison to other brides? Her perfect features, her lovely gown, her adornment, or the joy in her eyes as she gazed at her man? Now imagine Christ looking at us. He sees beyond the surface into the most hidden crannies of our hearts. Although we may look fine on the outside, God knows the truth. If we truly love Him and live in obedience to His Word, we will be beautiful to Him.

We women long to be beautiful. This longing can make us prone to follow the latest fads and fashions. Maybe we say, "I don't want to look like an old grandma!" or "What's wrong with this hairstyle?" We need to look beneath the surface and examine ourselves honestly. Ask, "Am I doing this to win my friends' approval or to get attention from men? Do I believe God is honored by a short or form-fitting skirt or a low neckline?" Remember, God sees inside our hearts and knows our motives and desires, even if we restrain ourselves from following the crowd outwardly.

God wants to adorn us with the ornament He highly prizes—a meek and quiet spirit (1 Peter 3:4). Instead of flaunting ourselves before others or even subconsciously trying to draw eyes to our appearance, we will honor and reverence God and avoid anything that causes men to struggle in their thoughts. Are you seeking to be a beautiful bride in Christ's eyes? Ask God to give you true beauty so you can be the woman He wants you to be.

Dear Lord, I want to portray the ornament of a meek and quiet spirit, reverencing both my husband and you. Thank you for loving me and for enlightening me through your Word. In Jesus' name, Amen.

The beauty that you often see
　Is indiscreet and bold.
Far better is the humble grace
　That in your heart you hold.

When Christ resides within your heart,
　With godliness you'll shine,
You'll make His way attractive,
　Showing holiness divine.

Oh, will you seek the beauty true
　Which God alone bestows?
You'll find wholeness and purity
　And joy His children know.

Scripture reading: Colossians 3:18–24; Titus 2:3–5

God's Plan Is Best

Some call the woman the heart of the home. Even if a mother doesn't always feel organized or on top of things, she still sets the tone in the home. When she grumbles, the children mope too. If she belittles her husband, the children regard him with less respect. When she fails to support her husband, her children also ignore his wishes. The whole family misses a blessing when the wife usurps God's plan. When young people absorb contempt for authority in the home, they bring that attitude to their relationships with other authority in the church or in society.

God calls the man the head of the home (1 Corinthians 11:3). Sometimes men don't lead as they should, to the detriment of the family. We wives can empower our husbands by looking to them for leadership, encouraging them to take their responsibility seriously. When the father shoulders Christlike authority in the home, security and peace can flourish.

As the heart of the home, you must be sensitive to your children's emotional needs. Share these needs with your husband and pray together for direction. You teach your children best by example. Can you tell them the Bible says, "Children, obey your parents," (Ephesians 6:1) if you neglect to submit to your husband (Ephesians 5:22)?

Does the job seem daunting? Your roles as a godly woman, a wife, and a mother entail great responsibility. But take heart! You have the greatest Source of strength at your side. As you depend upon Christ to help you, He will bless you beyond our expectations. Take your God-ordained place with a happy heart, dear sister. His plan is best!

Dear Lord, help me to honor my husband, to recognize the needs in my family, and to persevere in prayer. I claim your strength. In Jesus' name, Amen.

The choice is yours to yield your will,
    Submitting to your head,
Or take the stubborn way and find
    All joy in Christ has fled.

O can we see God's way is best?
    For He has planned it so
To make our home a blessed place
    Where love and peace can grow.

So be a woman God approves,
    And give Him all your heart;
He offers grace for every day
    And strength to do your part.

Returning Christ's Love

Christ's love for the church compelled Him to leave the glory of heaven. He agonized in Gethsemane, sweating as it were great drops of blood (Luke 22:44). He endured mocking and scourging. And then, love took Him to Calvary. Jesus suffered a horrible death on a cross to purchase His pure, spotless bride.

Have we heard this story so often that we take it for granted? God forbid! We can never repay our debt to Christ, but our love for Him should grow with the passage of time.

So how do we show Him our love? By living for Him, not for ourselves (2 Corinthians 5:15). We should pray daily, "Lord, help me to please you today, to honor you as my Lord and Savior." We must love Christ more than anyone or anything else. He chose us "that we should be holy and without blame before him in love" (Ephesians 1:4). Our faithfulness to Him wafts upward like a sweet perfume.

As part of Christ's bride, we must live in joyful obedience to Him, having put off the old man and put on the new man (Ephesians 4:22–24). This is love in action. We look forward to the fulfillment of this promise: "When Christ, who is our life, shall appear, then shall ye also appear with him in glory" (Colossians 3:4).

Is your love for your heavenly Bridegroom evident? Do others know you are eagerly awaiting His return? Are you speaking of Him and to Him daily? Are you ready for Christ to come and catch you away to be with Him forever?

"O how I love you, precious bride,
　　So beautiful and kind;
Your reverent spirit pleases me;
　　I am so glad you're mine.

"Your shining garment, pure and white,
　　Declares your purity;
I see your faith, obedience,
　　And deep humility.

"Soon I'm coming back for you;
　　I'll take you home with me;
We'll never part again, dear love;
　　We're one eternally."

A Sure Foundation

Whom do we trust? We trust the bank that invests our money, the electric company that supplies us with power, the mechanic who fixes our vehicle, and the grocer who sells us food. We trust our doctors, often placing our lives in their hands.

Trust forms the bedrock that undergirds relationships. Without trust in a marriage, its walls will fracture and crumble. When trust has been broken, it takes much time to rebuild.

A marriage, like a sturdy house, must begin with the sure foundation of both partners living in close fellowship with God. Christ must be our Cornerstone, the firm, enduring Rock on which we construct our relationship.

Trust in marriage is strengthened by faithfulness and respect. Never entertain the idea of flirting with someone else. Keep your thoughts pure and your love focused on each other and God.

Trust is also built through sacrificial love, putting the other first without grumbling, even if it means changing your own plans. Dependability builds trust; neglect of duty threatens it. When your husband comes home weary and hungry, can he depend on you to have a meal ready for him, welcoming him with affection? Can he trust you to care for the family in his absence? Do your children see love and trust between their parents as you love and honor God?

Satan wants to erode trust between marriage partners, but "[God] is a shield unto them that put their trust in him" (Proverbs 30:5). We must be diligent and alert to any threats to our marriages. At the first sign of trouble, seek God's direction.

Are there any cracks in the walls of your marriage? Cry out to God, and seek godly counsel. God wants to strengthen your marriage, and He has given us a support system through godly older individuals in our churches. May your marriage be blessed as you build on Christ, our sure foundation.

Dear Lord, thank you for showing us in your Word how to build our marriages. Help me to be trustworthy. In Jesus' name, Amen.

Together we will look to God,
 And seek His will to do.
We'll love the Lord, each other too,
 And to our vows be true.
Upon the Rock we'll build our home;
 With this foundation sure
Our love will stand the storms of life;
 Our marriage will endure.

Pink Walls and Appreciation

How exciting to plan our wedding and decorate our first home! My husband-to-be rented an old farmhouse, and we began cleaning and painting.

"I'd like antique white paint for the dining room," I told him. Imagine my surprise that weekend when I walked into the house and was welcomed by pink walls! "Why did you buy pink paint?" I exclaimed, frowning.

"Mom picked up the paint for me. She said she knew you wanted antique white paint, but she thought pink would make it more cheery. It's okay, isn't it?" he asked warily.

"But it's our house! We should have the say about what we do."

"I know, but how do we tell my mom that? She probably doesn't think we are as experienced as she is."

I sighed. "I guess so, but *pink* walls?"

That night I poured out my woes to my mother. She gave me some advice: "Look, it is just paint. The next time you need to paint, you can do it yourself. Until then, smile and thank her for helping. Let her know you appreciate what she has done for you. Choose to honor her as your mother-in-law. Begin now to build a relationship of respect. After all, you're marrying her son. Swallow your disappointment, and learn to love her." And I did.

Love helps us to bear with others' faults or offenses. Instead of insisting on our own way, we will choose God's way of meekness. This carries a great responsibility; our response may influence that person to either accept or reject the love of Jesus. Will we love as Jesus does?

We have no greater gift to offer than our love. Through love we point others to the author of love—our heavenly Father.

> *Dear Lord, help me to love as you have loved and to take your way, not mine. Forgive me for my selfishness, and give me grace to put others first. In Jesus' name, Amen.*

It's up to us to choose each day
　　The path on which we go;
Will we deny our sinful self,
　　Or choose the path of woe?

The Lord will give us grace to walk
　　The path of love each day,
To set aside the reign of self,
　　And choose the Savior's way.

Hanging Pictures

The time had come to decorate our new home. We gathered pictures and plaques for the living room. My husband, hammer and nails in hand, surveyed the room.

"I think this picture would look nice over there." I pointed to the spot.

"No, it should go over here." Swiftly, the nail went in and the picture went up. Each time my suggestions were ignored.

"Since you don't need my help, I'll unpack some more boxes." Stung, I left the room. *Will it always be like this?* I wondered, self-pity rising inside me. *I guess it's just his house, not ours.* I treated my husband rather coolly the rest of the day, feeding my injured pride.

He apologized later in the day when he realized what he had done. "I want us to be a team." His words soothed me. I apologized, too, for assuming I was in charge. I had expected he wouldn't care enough to get involved. I had thought he would say, "Just tell me where to hang it." The situation had shone a spotlight on our pride—his in thinking that his way was always best, and mine in believing my idea was better. How young and foolish we were! Relationships matter more than where pictures are hung, but we often major on the minors, as the saying goes.

In Nebuchadnezzar's case, God used drastic measures to bring down the king's arrogance. God still hates pride (Proverbs 8:13). When we recognize pride in our lives, we must confess it and ask God to help us put it to death. We find deliverance as we humble ourselves at the feet of Jesus in this way. Asking forgiveness from those we have offended brings restoration and healing.

Dear Lord, forgive me and cleanse me of pride so I can please you. In Jesus' name, Amen.

Let thy grace, Lord, make me lowly,
Humble all my swelling pride;
Fallen, guilty, and unholy,
Greatness in my eyes I'll hide:
I'll forbid my vain aspiring,
Nor at earthly honors aim,
No ambitious heights desiring,
Far above my humble claim.

—William Goode

The Flopped Pie

Blissfully in love with each other, a newlywed couple often expects to cruise through married life like a car on a smooth highway. Thus the potholes of adjustment take them by surprise, causing hurt feelings.

Soon after our wedding, my husband asked for pie. I prepared a pie using a filling he had bought. That evening he eagerly served himself a large piece of pie. To my dismay, juice ran all over. "Well, it's really juicy," he remarked and took a big bite. "What's wrong with this pie? Didn't you use any sugar?"

"No, pie filling is already sweetened." I retrieved the empty can from the wastebasket. "This was just berries! You bought the wrong thing."

"Well, you should have realized that when you opened it. This pie isn't fit to eat! I'm going to throw it to the pig. Maybe next time you can do better."

"Who said I'd make another pie for you?" I cried hotly as he went out the door with the pie.

Marital bliss hit a huge bump! After a good cry, the Lord began to speak to me. "So your pie was a flop, but what about your feelings toward your husband? Will you resent his words, or admit that your inexperience helped cause the blunder?"

"Okay, Lord, I won't be angry. I'll try again." Wiping my tears, I whispered, "You'll eat my next pie, dear husband!"

Lloyd walked into the kitchen, eying me warily. Taking me in his arms, he apologized. "I'm sorry I hurt your feelings. I didn't mean to. But that pie was so sour! Even the pig won't eat it!" Then we began to laugh. Forgiveness restored our newlywed bliss.

My dad gave me this piece of advice, referencing Ephesians 4:26, "Never let the sun go down on your wrath. Always set things right before you go to bed. Then you can sleep in peace and never have regrets." Unless you make forgiveness an integral part of your marriage, your relationships with both your husband and God will suffer.

Jesus says if we refuse to forgive others, our Father will not forgive us (Matthew 6:15). Daily injustices fade in the light of eternity. Ask God for grace to forgive and live in peace.

Dear Lord, help me to practice love and forgiveness each day so that I have no regrets and so peace will reign in my heart and home. In Jesus' name, Amen.

O help us, Lord, each day to place
　　Our hurts into your hand,
Forgiving those who wound our hearts,
　　Obeying your command.

In the Doghouse

Not long after our wedding, we decided to pay a short visit to friends in another town. Soon after we arrived, the men drove to a garden plot our friends had rented. We expected them home shortly, but as it grew dark, we wondered, "What could be keeping them?" We jumped in the car to go look for them. When we arrived at the garden, we found them ready to leave. "What have you been doing all this time?" we questioned.

Quietly the answer came, "Praying." A mutual friend who needed encouragement had met up with them, and time had slipped away as they talked and prayed.

As my husband and I drove home, I still felt upset. Yes, I wanted them to be able to encourage our friend, but did it have to take several hours? I had seen very little of my husband that evening, and his absence had worried me. He should have insisted on leaving sooner. I fumed silently. My husband didn't say much either.

Arriving home, I went inside briskly and prepared for bed. I listened for my husband's steps, but heard only silence. *What is he doing outside so long?*

It seemed the Lord said, *"Why would he want to be in the house with an angry woman? You should be ashamed of yourself! What was most important tonight—you, or your friend's need?"*

Sobbing, I asked the Lord's forgiveness. Next I needed to find my husband. I opened the door, and called into the darkness. "Aren't you coming in?"

"I thought since I'm in the doghouse tonight, I might as well sit out here with Lucky [our dog]."

"I'm so sorry for my attitude. Won't you please come in? You're not in the doghouse anymore."

"Gladly!" he replied. Peace and love reigned once more.

When you are upset, take a step back and assess the situation. Could you be at fault too? Are your expectations unreasonable? When you bring it to the Lord, He reveals your heart. Remember, you can't have peace with God while living in conflict with others. "The fruit of righteousness is sown in peace of them that make peace" (James 3:18).

Dear Lord, I want you to reign in my life. I want to be quick to forgive and extend grace to others. I want to please you always. In Jesus' name, Amen.

Angry words! O let them never
From the tongue unbridled slip;
May the heart's best impulse ever
Check them ere they soil the lip.
—Horatio R. Palmer

How's the Atmosphere?

Have you ever walked into a home and felt tension in the atmosphere? Your hosts seemed uncomfortable, and you wondered, "Did I walk into the middle of an argument?"

The atmosphere in a home shapes the children who live there. If they see love and respect between their parents, they feel secure. In many cases, when discord arises, a child blames himself for the situation. As a wife, your response to conflict may become the method your children adopt. Do you believe your way is better than your husband's? Speaking your mind may not help matters; certainly not if it undermines your husband's authority.

Your children observe your relationship and often pattern their marriages after it, because they see your relationship as normal. You may say, "I'm not the only one to blame for tension in our home." Perhaps not, but you can do something about it if you're willing to pay the price. Laying down self will diminish strife. Praying for your husband and asking the Lord to help you love and respect him will also begin to clear the atmosphere.

When your husband senses God's love pouring out of you through deeds of kindness and submission, he no longer has to feel defensive. Allowing God to change you will change the way you interact with your husband. Pray, as David did, "Set a watch, O Lord, before my mouth; keep the door of my lips" (Psalm 141:3). God will help you.

Bathe your life with prayer. Look to God as your strength. Be a woman your husband can trust and depend upon. Bless your children with a home where God is honored, the wife is in her place, and the husband is reverenced. If the tense atmosphere in your home sends sparks flying, take steps today to diffuse the static—in God's way.

Dear Lord, help me to put self aside and to love and honor my husband. May our home be one of peace. In Jesus' name, Amen.

O Lord, please grant us wisdom pure,
　Your mercy, love, and grace;
That those who enter through our doors
　May sense Christ in this place.

Tornado Watch

Huddled in the basement, a baby in my arms and the other three children crouching around me, I listened for the sound of a tornado. The couple from next door had joined us, since their house had no basement, but still I felt alone.

I wished for my husband, but he had taken a trip with some other men to look at properties in another state. I silently called out to God, *Oh, God, be our shelter. Protect these little ones from harm. Help me to rest in you. Calm my fears so the children will not be afraid.* After sitting in the basement for several hours, the danger passed and our neighbors went home.

As we climbed the stairs, our oldest said, "Mom, I wish Dad were here."

"I do too, son." When we gathered for devotions, I missed my husband even more.

After prayers, I tucked the children into bed and sat down to rock the baby, thinking about how much I relied on my husband. He worked hard to support us, helped with gardening and childcare, led in family worship, and took us to church regularly. If I had a problem, he could usually fix it. I was greatly blessed!

I thought of widows and others who faced this loneliness every day, and I wondered how they could bear it. Again I prayed, "O Lord, be my shelter and my comfort."

What rejoicing there was in our little family when Daddy came home! We snuggled together on the living room sofa and each of the children recounted his version of our evening in the basement.

Fathers play such an important role in family life. Little boys try to do just as Daddy does. Daughters look to him for approval and assurance of his love. Wives feel secure with a husband who loves and cares for her and the children, and who loves God most of all.

God, our heavenly Father, is our anchor, our shelter, our help, and our hope. He gave us earthly fathers and husbands to give us a glimpse of His greater love for each of us. We can rest in His everlasting arms. Like a father, He loves and cares for His beloved children.

Dear Lord, thank you for being my shelter in the storms of life. Help me to trust in you at all times. You are a perfect Father! In Jesus' name, Amen.

Father and friend, thy light, thy love
Beaming through all thy works, we see
Thy glory gilds the heav'ns above,
And all the earth is full of thee.

Thy children shall not faint nor fear,
Sustained by this delightful tho't:
Since thou, their God, art ev'rywhere,
They cannot be where thou art not.

—John Bowring

The Love of Family

"The love of family is one of life's greatest gifts." The motto hanging on the wall portrayed this saying. Unfortunately not everyone enjoys a wonderful family life. Parents sometimes inflict great pain on their children. Rebellious sons and daughters bring sorrow to godly parents. Family members sometimes reject each other and lose touch for months or years. These broken family ties hurt. When one member stays away from a family gathering, our hearts ache. We want the missing person to return and be reconciled.

God also plans for us to enjoy closeness with a spiritual family—the church. Together we work to bring His erring children back into fellowship with Him and His people. The relationship we have with God through faith in His Son is so precious; He calls us His sons and daughters! We want all to go home someday to our heavenly Father. It grieves us to think of anyone missing this privilege.

Some people reject this relationship to their own hurt. Yet when we turn to God for forgiveness and healing, He gives us a desire to rebuild relationships with both our natural and our church families. Restoration is always God's plan. The prodigal's father in today's reading never lost hope that his son would return. Even so does our loving God wait for us with open arms.

The love of a family—whether natural or spiritual—is a gift. We should never take each other for granted. Every day as we pour out our hearts for them in prayer and love, we are raising a hedge of protection against Satan's fiery darts. How can we bless our families today?

Dear Lord, thank you for my natural and my spiritual family. Help me to appreciate and strengthen both. In Jesus' name, Amen.

People of the living God,
I have sought the world around;
Paths of sin and sorrow trod,
Peace and comfort nowhere found:
Now to you my spirit turns,
Turns a fugitive unblest;
Brethren, where your altar burns,
O, receive me into rest.

—James Montgomery

Loving Our Children

The wise King Solomon needed to judge between two women, both of whom claimed to be the mother of a baby. "Divide the child in half, giving half to each woman," he commanded.

"Give her the living child! Don't slay him!" came the agonized cry of one of the women.

"Divide him!" the other woman insisted.

King Solomon recognized true mother love and gave the child to the woman who valued her child's life above her rightful claim.

True love does what is best for our child. We give up ourselves—our own desires, time, and ambitions—to give our children what they need. They don't need expensive toys or clothing, but they do need parents who show them love and take time to listen to them.

True love means we lovingly discipline our children. Godly discipline yields good fruit: "The rod and reproof give wisdom: but a child left to himself bringeth his mother to shame" (Proverbs 29:15). "Correct thy son, and he shall give thee rest; yea, he shall give delight unto thy soul" (Proverbs 29:17).

Psalm 127:3 calls children "an heritage of the LORD"—gifts to treasure. Who they become depends largely upon us, which ought to sober us. God's Word must guide and instruct us in their training.

In today's world many clamoring voices seek to destroy the innocence and faith of our children. Women of God should weep for the children in our society, not only for all the aborted babies, but also for the children whose minds are being defiled and confused by parents and teachers. Things are transpiring that we never dreamed would happen. May our mother hearts be touched, and our prayers ascend for the children around us.

Teach your children and grandchildren to look to God's Word as the final and ultimate authority. Treasure and nurture the children in your life. Hold them close, and teach them to love God.

Dear Lord, help me to be a faithful mother in word and action. Give me grace to teach the children in my life to love you with all their hearts. Give me a burden of intercession for the children of this world.
In Jesus' name, Amen.

Our hearts are weeping, Father,
 For children of today
Who do not know of Jesus;
 O mothers, we must pray!

Ideals for Our Children

Who are your children's heroes? Many children look to television characters, sports figures, or music idols. They want someone to imitate and adore. Perhaps they say, "I want to be like Mom or Dad when I grow up." They look at parents or older siblings with admiration, love, and respect, and they want to follow their example. How sobering!

The Bible says Satan goes about like a raging lion seeking prey to devour. Dangling temptation in front of our children is one way he can entice them. Children need daily instruction and example to help them develop a firm faith in God. They must form solid convictions that will help protect them against the fascination of wickedness. Church attendance alone will not build in them the moral fiber they need. Sisters, we must be the older women who are examples of godliness for the children around us!

What children read also impacts their lives. I am concerned for our teenage girls who are reading so-called Christian novels. Many of these are slightly watered down romance stories which do not promote the high ideals we want for our daughters and granddaughters. Can we expect them to want to conform to our standards when they indulge in books that feed the flesh?

Are we giving our children books that inspire them to follow Christ? Hudson Taylor, missionary to China, grew up hearing his father reading and talking about China. At the age of four or five, Hudson declared when he was a man, he would be a missionary to China.[19] What we feed upon influences what we become.

As the saying goes, "More is caught than taught." This does not mean we needn't teach our children, but do they see us choosing to separate ourselves from the world? Do we get excited about politics or sports, or do we get excited about missions and church work? Do we pursue Christ above all else? Do we take time to pray, read, and meditate? Do we cultivate relationships with God's people? Can we tell our children what Paul told others? "Be ye followers of me, even as I also am of Christ." (1 Corinthians 11:1). This question should sober all parents and grandparents.

Children not only need to know that they are loved—by us and by God—but also that God hates sin. We have only a few short years to guide our children. Are we giving them principles by which to live, holding up Christ as our example, and living before them a conse-crated life? As children see our joy in the Lord, surely they will they want that too!

Dear Lord, help me to be an example that is safe for children to follow. In Jesus' name, Amen.

Today is mine to mold this child,
To teach him in Christ's way,
O help me, Lord, to never lead
This precious one astray.

Danger! Poison!

A box of poison sat on a high shelf out of the reach of the young child playing on the floor. His parents would never let him handle such a dangerous item. In the next room, however, their teenage daughter sat entranced by the figures on the screen in front of her. Fashions that displayed the body and drew attention, along with scenes of lewdness and immorality, captivated her eyes and heart. Her ears heard things no woman should hear. She was consuming poison as surely as if she had eaten from the box on her mother's shelf. This kind of poison invades and corrupts the mind, spreading its toxins throughout the entire body. Those who take in this poison become addicts, slaves to Satan.

Do you protect your family as much as possible from evil influences? You must constantly stay alert, because these influences sneak into your life almost unnoticed. Teach your children and grandchildren to flee from evil, and make sure your home is a safe place for them.

If you now have more leisure time, do you read things you wouldn't want your daughters or nieces to read? Maybe it is just a little over the line you set when you had teenagers in your home, but you think you can handle it. *After all,* Satan whispers, *You are mature enough to disregard the questionable parts. It won't affect you.*

The Holy Spirit whispers to your heart, *Danger! Poison!* A mature woman's mind is still susceptible to the seductive fantasies that lurk in a teenager's mind. Saturating your mind and theirs with God's Word builds a hedge of protection. God promises to shield to those who trust Him (Proverbs 30:5).

Remember, Jesus was tempted just as you are. He cares and He stands ready to help you. In your own strength (actually, weakness), you cannot withstand the enemy. You must depend upon the Lord.

> *Dear Lord, I want to protect and be protected against temptation and sin. Help me to be a strong example of godliness to younger women, and to have nothing in my life that would put a stumbling block in their path.*
> *In Jesus' name, Amen.*

Consider how the eyes and ears
    Give entrance to the soul,
How that which passes through the gates
    Will soon be in control.

We need to daily stay on guard,
    And pray with fervency.
The Lord will give us power to stand;
    Through Christ comes victory!

Precious in His Sight

A friend told me her young daughter dreamed of having a canopy bed, but they could not afford one. Unknown to the mother, however, her daughter was praying God would give her a canopy bed.

One day my friend seemed to hear an almost audible voice saying, "Buy a *Peddler's Post*."

"Why? I've never bought one." A day or so later, she again felt prompting to buy the paper, so she asked her son to bring one home.

Prayerfully she turned the pages and saw an ad for a canopy bed. The price exceeded their budget, but the ad offered everything they were looking for—bed and window curtains, even a bookcase and desk. They called the sellers and told them they were considering purchasing it.

But after more discussion, my friend told the owners they couldn't afford it. To her amazement, the seller lowered the price to two hundred dollars. "I'll talk to my husband about it," my friend replied. They decided to buy the bed. When they went to get it, the lady told them they had advertised the bed for a whole year and had received no calls. They prayed about it and decided that if someone called, they would reduce the price. Two prayers got answered, and God received the glory.

God had rewarded that little girl's faith. She felt His care. She realized

He sees her as precious. Since then, that memory has often encouraged her. When she questions her worth or feels discouraged, she remembers the day God answered her prayer of faith.

Do you ever wonder if God cares about you personally? If your longings and desires matter to Him? In today's reading, God calls His people precious. Those who believe in Christ belong to Him, and God cares about each of His children.

In the words of David, "How precious also are thy thoughts unto me, O God! How great is the sum of them! If I should count them, they are more in number than the sand: when I awake, I am still with thee" (Psalm 139:17–18). Never forget you are precious in God's sight. God cares about the desires of a little girl's heart—and yours too.

> *Dear Lord, thank you that I can know I am precious to you. I want to show my love and devotion to you, bringing glory to your name, and staying close to your side. In Jesus' name, Amen.*

Savior, hear us, we pray
Keep us safe through this day
Keep our lives free from sin,
And our hearts pure within.
Jesus, Lord, hear our prayer
May we rest in Thy care.

—W. W. Ellsworth

185

Lord, Be Merciful

When the Pharisee went up to the temple to pray, did he actually pray or did he just stroke his ego? The account in Luke 18 says "The Pharisee stood and prayed thus with himself" (v. 11). In trying to prove his own righteousness, he missed receiving God's forgiveness (v. 14).

The other man who went up to pray, a tax collector, had been rejected by society. Everyone knew these men often embezzled. His head bowed, he stood alone, beating his chest and praying fervently, "God, be merciful to me a sinner" (v. 13). He didn't try to convince God of his own goodness, he just acknowledged his sinfulness and begged the Lord for mercy. Jesus says "this man went down to his house justified," unlike the other man (v. 14). Why? Jesus goes on to explain, "for every one that exalteth himself shall be abased; and he that humbleth himself shall be exalted" (v. 14).

Which man do you most resemble? Do you sometimes think yourself better than others? Do you expect other people to come up to your social, spiritual, or personal standards? Do you think you're doing quite a bit for God? Perhaps you, too, can list your good deeds: serving on church committees, helping at a Christian school, hosting guests, volunteering at the nursing home, and baking cookies for busy mothers, the poor, and those in prison. Does your attitude bear any resemblance to the Pharisee's?

The self-promoting advertising all around us urges, "Buy this—you deserve it." Even birthday cards say, "You deserve to have the best." Our society pressures women to do whatever it takes to assure their happiness and success, even at the expense of their families. In contrast, Jesus wants us to have a humble attitude, to seek His will for our lives, and to accept with gratefulness whatever He deems best for us.

How often do we need to come to God, crying out, "Lord, be merciful to me a sinner"? None of us can claim perfection. We all must cast ourselves upon the mercy of a just and loving God.

Dear Lord, I have nothing of which to brag. I need your grace and mercy every day so I can walk humbly before you. In Jesus' name, Amen.

The Lord of all sees in our hearts;
He knows the sin in every part.
He gladly hears the heart that cries,
"O save me, Lord, or I will die!"

The Place to Find Wisdom

*J*ob, the ancient sage, asks, "But where shall wisdom be found? And where is the place of understanding?" (Job 28:12). Later in the same passage, he gives the answer: "Behold, the fear of the LORD, that is wisdom; and to depart from evil is understanding" (v. 28).

James 3:13–18 gives us a checklist to see if we have God's kind of wisdom, and if our lives show its fruit. Do we speak in meekness or do we seek the applause of men? Do we show humility, even when we are misused? Do we stir up strife or harbor envy? Do we retaliate when others wrong us, or do we seek peace? God's kind of wisdom "is first pure, then peaceable, gentle and easy to be intreated, full of mercy and good fruits, without partiality, and without hypocrisy" (v. 17).

How do we respond when someone approaches us with a word of correction? Can we receive it with humility? True wisdom conducts itself with gentleness. Why would we close our minds and hearts to appeal from those who seek our spiritual wellbeing?

Wisdom gives us grace to show impartiality in our thinking and our actions, treating all people as important in God's eyes. We will stand for truth and righteousness and show mercy to others.

Christians have often been accused of hypocrisy. Our actions count more than our words; no one sees this more clearly than our children. May it be said of us as of the Proverbs 31 woman, "She openeth her mouth with wisdom; and in her tongue is the law of kindness" (v. 26). Verses 4 and 5 of today's Scripture say if we seek wisdom as diligently as one would seek silver or hidden treasures, we will come to fear and know God. Then we will shun evil and will fear and love our heavenly Father.

Are you seeking true wisdom from above?

Dear Lord, help me seek your wisdom and understanding. Give me grace to live to bring forth fruit to glorify you. In Jesus' name, Amen.

O grant us light, that we may know
The wisdom Thou alone canst give;
That truth may guide where'er we go,
And virtue bless where'er we live.[k]

—Lawrence Tuttiett

[k] *Hymns of the Church,* #996A.

A Pure Heart

The charge nurse carefully wrapped a blanket around the tiny newborn and carried him into the room at the end of the hall. His mother, an unwed teenager, would soon be discharged, but her little son would stay behind. She had one hour to hold him before they would be separated, perhaps forever.

She cradled the baby in her arms, tears running down her cheeks. After carrying this baby for nine months and giving birth to a strong, healthy child, her heart brimmed with love for him. I imagine she was thinking, *How can I give him up?* Her parents had insisted she give him up for adoption so she could get on with her life. How heartbreaking to see the grief experienced in severing this maternal bond! Yet it is even more disturbing to see young women birthing a second or third child, nonchalantly putting them up for adoption because they don't want a baby restricting their lifestyle.

As I worked in the maternity hospital, I observed these young mothers, many of them still in high school, and my heart went out to them. Their lives had been changed forever by a choice they made nine months earlier. Had they not been taught the value of chastity or the blessing of keeping oneself pure for a future husband? Today many women view abortion as a natural choice or a right they have. Squandering purity outside marriage always brings regrets. God will forgive our trespasses, but painful consequences follow.

Solomon counsels, "My son, give me thine heart, and let thine eyes observe my ways" (Proverbs 23:26). He goes on to warn his son of the dangers of immorality. God, our Father, also says, "Give me your heart." He wants us to love Him more than anyone or anything, desiring to please Him most of all. When God says no to something, He says it for our good.

In this day when immorality has taken on epidemic proportions, we must stay on guard and keep our hearts and lives pure to avoid Satan's trap. What we read or watch opens us to temptations that lead to choices. Paul wrote to Timothy, "Flee also youthful lusts: but follow righteousness, faith, charity, peace, with them that call on the Lord out of a pure heart" (2 Timothy 2:22). Only in Christ do we find real victory and freedom.

God calls us to a life of purity and commitment to Him. He longs to direct our steps. He has the perfect plan for our lives—a path that abounds with blessing and joy—if we will listen to Him and follow His directions.

Dear Lord, I give you my heart. Help me to depend on you when temptations come. In Jesus' name, Amen.

O Holy Spirit, keep us pure,
Grant us thy strength when sins allure;
Our bodies are thy temple, Lord;
Be thou in thought and act adored.

—Adelaide Mary Plumptre

Road Closed Ahead

On the road to a town in another part of the state, my husband and I encountered a roadblock. Barriers blocked the next two roads as well. Changing our plans, we traveled yet farther to find an open road going north.

We experience roadblocks in our spiritual lives too. Perhaps we think we have our life planned out. We think, *Here is what I'm going to do. This is what I want to accomplish in life.* Then things don't work out as we had hoped. We're brought up short, and we wonder why.

In the face of disappointment, I ought to consider: Did I first pray about my plans? Am I seeking God's will—or my own desires? Am I willing to surrender my plans to God and His timing?

A "Road Closed Ahead" sign blocks the way for a good reason. In our case, the railroad was being repaired. God faithfully sets warning signs in our path, and His reasons are always good. Some ignore the cautions of godly counsel to their own hurt: "The way of a fool is right in his own eyes: but he that hearkeneth unto counsel is wise" (Proverbs 12:15).

Not every roadblock is from God; sometimes Satan is trying to keep us from something that would bring glory to the Lord's kingdom. We need to carefully consider the thing that is hindering us and bring it to God in prayer, asking Him to clearly show us His will in this circumstance. He is faithful and will answer—sometimes *Go*, sometimes *Stop*, and sometimes *Wait.*

Take heed to the warnings God places in your path. Do they warn of danger ahead? Listen to God's counsel. Pray diligently, and seek His will. If you feel uncertain about a decision you must make, search God's Word for direction, pray, and seek counsel of a godly person. Remember, God wants the best for you, as these verses show: "In the way of righteousness is life: and in the pathway thereof there is no death" (Proverbs 12:28). "Trust in the LORD with all thine heart; and lean not unto thine own understanding. In all thy ways acknowledge him, and he shall direct thy paths" (Proverbs 3:5–6). Walk in the way of righteousness, and God will preserve your way.

Dear Lord, help me to heed the warnings you give me so I will stay on the pathway that leads to life. In Jesus' name, Amen.

Teach me, O Lord, thy way of truth,
And from it I will not depart;
That I may steadfastly obey,
Give me an understanding heart.

—Psalter

True Happiness

For many people, happiness is like trying to catch a butterfly—it flutters above their reach, just when they think they have grasped it. People constantly seek to fill the God-shaped void within them. When they can't, they grow disillusioned with life.

Happiness for the unbeliever is uncertain, short-lived, and limited to this life: "The triumphing of the wicked is short, and the joy of the hypocrite is but for a moment" (Job 20:5).

True happiness comes only from God, as the psalmist says, "Blessed [happy or fortunate] is every one that feareth the LORD; that walketh in his ways" (Psalm 128:1). Proverbs 16:20 restates this theme: "Whoso trusteth in the LORD, happy is he."

Should Christians reach for happiness, or should we seek after joy? The difference between the two is what source it comes from. Circumstances will not affect a Christian's joy. Even in suffering or persecution, our joy in Christ will not dissipate because it resides deep in our souls. It is an inner confidence that Jesus has redeemed us from sin and its power over us and that He will never forsake us. Joy radiates from our countenances. Earthly happiness, in contrast, is a feeling brought on by a set of events and is therefore fleeting. Now we feel it—now we don't. Unbelievers are constantly searching for happiness in possessions, places, or people, only to be disappointed. Unlike them, we have this promise: "Blessed are they which do hunger and thirst after righteousness: for they shall be filled" (Matthew 5:6). When we seek God, He will not disappoint us. He is waiting to fill us with great joy and contentment. In God, we find all we need. He satisfies our deepest longings.

Dear Lord, thank you for the joy I find when I trust in you. Help me to share with others this promise of deep, abiding joy. In Jesus' name, Amen.

O happy is the woman
Who walks with God each day;
She takes the time to listen,
To hear His voice, to pray.

O happy is the woman
Who in the Lord delights;
She seeks to do His pleasure,
And to uphold the right.

O happy is the woman
Who rests in Christ each day;
She waits in trust and patience;
God is her strength and stay.

O happy is the woman
Whose hope is fixed above;
She looks unto the Savior,
And revels in His love.

Scripture reading: Ephesians 4:17–32

What Are You Wearing?

A new outfit! What woman doesn't smile at the thought? She may have bought it at a fancy boutique or a thrift shop, or she may have sewn it herself. In any case, it cost her something.

The prophet Isaiah, however, speaks of a garment you can receive free of cost if you will ask for it: "I will greatly rejoice in the LORD, my soul shall be joyful in my God; for he hath clothed me with the garments of salvation, he hath covered me with the robe of righteousness" (Isaiah 61:10). God offers us "the garment of praise for the spirit of heaviness" (Isaiah 61:3).

When we get a new dress, the rest of our wardrobe looks shabbier by comparison. We might think, *I need a new pair of shoes to wear with this dress.* When we come to Christ and put on His robe of righteousness, we feel like a new person—because we are. We see the filthiness of our old garments—selfishness, anger, impurity, jealousy—and we want to cast them away forever. Colossians 3:5–8 instructs us to do just that. Later in the same passage, the Apostle Paul lists the lovely robes God has designed for us to wear: compassion, kindness, humility, meekness, patience, forbearance, love, peace, and thankfulness (vv. 12–15). These garments never go out of style, never wear out, befit every occasion, and enhance our appearance. We should eagerly clothe ourselves in them! What woman would not want to wear them?

Proverbs 31:25 mentions two more garments worth obtaining—strength and honor. God's store never closes or sells out. He stocks an infinite inventory, all free for the asking.

The saying goes, "Clothes define a person." So what kind of person do we want to portray? Do our physical clothes identify us as godly women who honor Him? When we are wearing Christ's garments, we will want our outer apparel to coordinate with our inner. Do you need a new dress or accessories? Place a call to Christ. He will gladly supply all you need.

> *Dear Lord, I want to be clothed with your righteousness*
> *and put on all the accessories you provide so I am ready*
> *when you return. Help me to throw away the filthy*
> *garments of my old life and never look back.*
> *In Jesus' name, Amen.*

The Bride eyes not her garment,
But her dear Bridegroom's face;
I will not gaze at glory,
But on my King of grace,
Not at the crown He giveth,
But on His pierced hand.
The Lamb is all the glory
Of Immanuel's land.[1]

—Annie R. Cousin

[1] "The Sands of Time Are Sinking," v. 4, *Hymns of the Church*, #720.

Behind the Door

As I opened the cupboard door, a stash of newspapers, magazines, cards, and letters slid toward me. I turned to my mother, whom I was helping with some deep cleaning. "Are you saving these things for some reason, Mom?"

"Oh, I suppose most of it could be thrown away. It's really just clutter, isn't it? Save anything important, and get rid of the rest." So I sorted through the stack, ending with a small stack of letters and a magazine of poetry.

How often do we clutter our minds with unnecessary or useless thoughts? Or our hearts by clinging to things we don't want to surrender to Christ? Years ago I heard a song entitled "The Shelf Behind the Door,"[20] a metaphor for the hidden place where a person kept hurt feelings, grudges, and unkind thoughts. Though the person knew it was wrong, she kept those thoughts and feelings in storage for a while, hoping God would not see. How foolish to try to hide things from our all-seeing God! He wants us to relinquish such clutter to Christ and find forgiveness and healing.

David expresses this reality when he says, "O God, thou knowest my foolishness: and my sins are not hid from thee" (Psalm 69:5). God sees our sin while it is still a thought; and it always separates us from Him. When we confess that sin, Christ advocates on our behalf with the Father, who forgives our sins.

Jesus says, "For nothing is secret, that shall not be made manifest; neither any thing hid, that shall not be known and come abroad" (Luke 8:17). If you are trying to hide things from God, you can be assured they will be exposed to the world on Judgment Day—if not before. Why not bring them to Christ now? Then you won't need a "shelf behind the door."

Welcome the Lord today, allowing Him to walk through every room of your mind. He sees all the clutter there, and He wants to clean it out. Let Him cleanse you and fill you with His peace and presence. You will experience a freedom you have never known.

Dear Lord, please help me spring clean my soul with your precious blood so I don't have worthless, dusty old grudges or hurts hidden inside. In Jesus' name, Amen.

Lord Jesus, I long to be perfectly whole;
I want thee forever to live in my soul;
Break down every idol, cast out ev'ry foe:
Now wash me, and I shall be whiter than snow.

Lord Jesus, look down from Thy throne in the skies,
And help me to make a complete sacrifice;
I give up myself and whatever I know:
Now wash me, and I shall be whiter than snow.

—James Nicholson

Scripture reading: Ephesians 3:8–21

Garage Sale Today

I stepped into the house, both hands carrying bags bursting with my finds. I had spent the whole day at garage sales and had found some great bargains. Items someone else had deemed useless met a need my family had. Yes, I felt weary, but pleased with my prizes.

Do we expend as much energy in searching out the treasures in God's Word? Do we exclaim over the nuggets of truth, the promises of God that so aptly address our needs for today and tomorrow? Do we share with our neighbors and friends the precious words we have found? These treasures far outlast any garage sale bargain. God's Word has ministered to mankind since the beginning of time.

We don't have to worry about outgrowing these treasures. They never become outdated, unusable, or rusty. They will never become unneeded clutter. The truths of God's Word apply to all generations and all peoples of the world. In fact, we ought to prize God's Word above all else, for it holds the secret to eternal life. The Bible offers hope to all who will heed its words. It shows us the way to a relationship with God through His Son Jesus Christ. What could be better?

Earthly things will decay and lose value, but Christ offers us eternal riches—the only true treasures. The Apostle Paul exhorts Timothy to warn the wealthy not to trust in the unreliable riches of this world (see 1 Timothy 6). Rather, he says, to "trust . . . in the living God, who giveth us richly all things to enjoy (v. 17). He instructs us to "be rich in good works," storing up treasures in heaven (v. 18).

Hold lightly the treasures found in this world, for they won't last long. Pursue earnestly and grasp tightly the greatest treasure! Dig deeply in His Word today!

> *Dear Lord, help me to think beyond these earthly things, to seek you and the treasures in your Word. Help me to cherish the jewels of truth that will help me through life and prepare me for eternity. I want to treasure you above all.*
> *In Jesus' name, Amen.*

O wonderful, wonderful Word of the Lord!

True wisdom its pages unfold;

And though we may read them a thousand times o'er,

They never, no never, grow old!

Each line hath a treasure, each promise a pearl,

That all if they will may secure;

And we know that when time and the world pass away,

God's Word shall forever endure.

—Fanny Crosby

If You Want Greatness

The mother of two of Jesus' followers came to Him with a request. "Allow my two sons to sit on either side of you in your kingdom."

Jesus asked, "Can you drink the same cup I will drink?" He referred to the suffering and death ahead of Him.

"Oh, yes," they answered. (Did they have any idea what they were saying?) Jesus knew the future, but He told them the coveted positions of honor were not His to grant.

The arrogance of James and John upset the other disciples. Perhaps they secretly wished they had thought to ask for the same favor. Jesus explained that the Gentiles had rulers and leaders who used their position to dominate others. He went on to say, "But it shall not be so among you: but whosoever will be great among you, let him be your minister; and whosoever will be chief among you, let him be your servant" (verses 26–27).

The natural urge to have power over others reminds me of the children's game called "King of the Mountain." As long as you can keep your position on top of the hill, you will remain king. You do whatever it takes—push, kick, threaten. Human nature shoves others out of the way to climb the ladder of success.

Christ's kingdom operates differently. Jesus told Pilate, "My kingdom is not of this world" (John 18:36). Throughout His life, Christ lived as a servant. He preached, prayed, healed, and fed the people,

202

even when He was weary and hungry. He served humanity without regard to individual position or wealth. At Calvary He displayed the ultimate expression of servanthood by giving His life to ransom us. Jesus told His disciples, "This is my commandment, that ye love one another, as I have loved you. Greater love hath no man than this, that a man lay down his life for his friends" (John 15:12–13).

True greatness sacrifices itself for others in obedience and love for our Master, seeking His approval. It means doing to others as we would to Jesus. Laying down self and donning the mantle of a servant brings glory to our Lord.

Dear Lord, help me to lay aside my pride and ambition and love you with all my heart. I want to be a joyful servant. In Jesus' name, Amen.

O Master, let me walk with Thee
In lowly paths of service free;
Tell me thy secret, help me bear
The strain of toil, the fret of care.

Teach me thy patience; still with thee
In closer, dearer company,
In work that keeps faith sweet and strong,
In trust that triumphs over wrong.

—Washington Gladden

203

Learning from Life's Experiences

My husband and I had just celebrated our fiftieth wedding anniversary with family and friends. Then I stumbled on a big rock in the dark, lost my balance, and ended up with a broken shoulder. I wondered, *Why, Lord?* I was still recovering from the open heart surgery I had undergone a few months previously.

God uses times like these to perfect us. He knows us intimately. He sees our failings even when we don't, so He gently reveals to us how much more we need to grow into His likeness.

Through these challenges, God taught me that I'm not in control—He is. Depending on others while I was laid up humbled me. All my adult life, I had taken care of others. Now I couldn't even comb my own hair!

I also learned to treasure my husband more. His unfailing kindness meant so much as he helped me with whatever I needed. This trying time deepened our relationship.

Our Scripture reading speaks of God trying us by allowing us to go through affliction. In the end He brings us to deeper maturity, fuller joy. Do we believe God knows best?

Surrendering to God's purposes and allowing Him to use us for His glory brings untold joy. Isn't that why He created us in the first place? Paul prays that believers would live in such a way "that the name of our

Lord Jesus Christ may be glorified in you, and ye in him, according to the grace of our God, and the Lord Jesus Christ" (2 Thessalonians 1:12).

Don't be discouraged by life's troublesome experiences, but see what God wants to teach you. Learn to glorify God in the midst of difficult circumstances. Thank Him for loving you enough to allow trials to purify and perfect you into His likeness.

Dear Lord, help me to learn the lessons you want to teach me. Thank you for knowing me so well and yet loving me so much. In Jesus' name, Amen.

Look deeper than the troubles
    Which seem to come your way;
Allow the Lord to mold you
    As the potter does the clay.
The beauty of the vessel
    Increases with the heat;
The Lord, our Master Potter;
    Will work a wondrous feat.

Blooming Where God Places You

Have you ever told yourself, "If circumstances were different I could be a vibrant Christian"? Do you find it challenging to bloom where God has placed you?

Consider how others have responded to undesirable circumstances. Joseph, when sold into slavery by his jealous brothers, could have sulked in useless bitterness (see Genesis 37). Instead, he accepted his lot with grace and stalwart faith, and God used him mightily to help entire nations.

Daniel, too, was ripped away from his family and homeland, but he remained true to God even when it looked like lions would shred him (see Daniel 6). His faithfulness led the pagan king Darius to mandate "that men should tremble and fear before the God of Daniel: for he is the living God, and stedfast forever" (v. 26).

Fanny Crosby, the blind hymn writer, did not allow bitterness or anger to stint her love for Christ. She devoted herself to God. As her love for the Savior grew deeper, her praise to Him burst forth in the eight thousand-plus hymns she penned for God's glory.[21] Her songs still inspire many.

Are you thriving in the soil where God has planted you, or are you just barely surviving? Do you submit to God's loving care, allowing Him to cultivate the ground of your heart, breaking up the clods of self-pity, regret, bitterness, and envy? Are you sending your roots deep into the Word of God? Do you lift your head to receive His blessings of sunshine and rain so you can bloom and bring forth fruit for His glory?

The Master Gardener will care for you well, no matter where you find yourself. As Psalm 92:13 says, "Those that be planted in the house of the LORD shall flourish in the courts of our God." When others see you thriving and blossoming even in harsh conditions, they will be drawn to Christ.

Dear Lord, I don't want to be a weak, whining Christian. I want to thrive and bloom for you. Please help me submit to you, trusting in your grace and mercy in every circumstance. In Jesus' name, Amen.

Resist the drought; lift up your head,
    And drink of heaven's dew.
The Lord has plenteous grace for you,
    And He will see you through.

In His Garden

Only a few months had passed since my mother's surgery for a malignant brain tumor. The operation had left her unable to communicate. I deeply missed the mother I had known before this devastating blow. We had always been close, sharing our joys and concerns with each other.

One day I placed my infant son in my mother's arms. He had been born the same week she had her brain surgery, in the same hospital. I watched as she cuddled my baby, and realized that she was still the same loving person she had always been, even though she couldn't express that love verbally. The inner beauty of her soul still flowered gently, silently, for the Master Gardener.

What about the garden of my heart? I pondered. *Can I accept what has happened to my precious mother? Will I be able to bloom through the trials I experience?* I had already lost my father, grandparents, a brother, and my own twin babies. And now this.

I knew people who became bitter, unforgiving, and withdrawn when life handed them difficulties. I didn't want to become one of them. So I asked the Master Gardener to weed my heart's garden, pulling weeds of discontentment and bitterness. Then the flowers of peace, joy, love, and thankfulness could bloom profusely. I chose to focus on my blessings and to look to Jesus as my all in all.

Years have passed and much has changed since that day I placed my infant son in his silent grandmother's arms, but God remains the same. He still shelters me when life's storms whip around me and He tends the garden of my heart with loving care. Every time I feel a weed of selfishness or anger cropping up, I call on Him. His tender cultivation encourages the flowers of His love to bloom.

The Lord will attend to your heart, too, if you ask. With the Lord in control, your heart will bloom with a sweet perfume of praise, glorifying Him.

Dear Lord, I ask you to be the Gardener of my heart. Pull out all the weeds that would keep me from being the beautiful flower you want me to be. May the beauty of Jesus be seen in me so you will be glorified. In Jesus' name, Amen.

Let the beauty of Jesus be seen in me,
All His wonderful passion and purity;
O my Savior divine, all my being refine,
Till the beauty of Jesus be seen in me.

—Albert Orsborn

A Pattern of Good Works

If you've ever sewn a dress, you know the importance of a suitable pattern. If you use the wrong pattern, your clothing will not fit, and you will have wasted the fabric. Similarly, your life serves as a pattern that influences the choices of people around you. You have the potential to guide others toward God or away from Him.

My mother lived as a pattern that led others to God. A few years ago we attended a funeral in my hometown. When a woman there heard my mother's name, she exclaimed, "Oh, I loved that dear lady! Do you know what she did for my husband and me?" She then told me her story.

This woman and her fiancé wanted to get married, but both their families were struggling financially. The couple decided to invite a few guests and not hold a reception. The groom's mother worked with my mother, and she told Mom about the situation. Mom's heart went out to the young couple, so she decided to help by purchasing a few items and baking a cake.

"I wasn't a Christian at that time, but your mother's example made me want to be one," the woman told me.

Hearing of my mother's loving gift to this couple—despite her own meager resources—didn't surprise me. Throughout my life, I had witnessed her kind deeds and sacrificial giving.

Recently I met another woman who related a kindness done by my mother. As a young girl, this woman had made looped hot pads to sell, but no one was buying them. Almost at the point of tears, this girl stopped at our house, and my mother bought all the hot pads she had. She said, "I've never forgotten what your mother did for me that day. She brought a smile back to my face." Even small deeds of kindness can bless people for a long time.

Dear sister, does your life provide a pattern that others can safely follow? Can they see Jesus in you? Do you live out your faith in practical ways that attract others to the Savior? Live as a true example of Christ so you will not lead others astray.

Dear Lord, I see my need to be a better example. Help me love as you love so I can be an excellent pattern for others to follow. In Jesus' name, Amen.

O to be like Thee! full of compassion,
Loving, forgiving, tender and kind,
Helping the helpless, cheering the fainting,
Seeking the wand'ring sinner to find.

O to be like Thee! O to be like Thee!
Blessed Redeemer, pure as Thou art.
Come in Thy sweetness; come in Thy fullness;
Stamp Thine own image deep on my heart.

—Thomas O. Chisholm

Scripture reading: 2 Peter 1:1–11

The Grace of Patience

"How long do you process vegetable soup in a water bath canner?" someone once asked me. She had purchased the ingredients, but she didn't have a pressure canner. I told her to cook the soup three hours since it contained meat. Later she showed me her row of attractively filled jars. "I cooked them only one and a half hours, but they all sealed." A few weeks later, however, lids began popping. She ended up throwing out all the soup. Because of impatience, she had nothing to show for her efforts.

We live in a society of impatient people, an age of one-minute meals and same-day deliveries. When we want something, we want it right now. Haven't we often told our children, "Just be patient"? We try to explain to them why they must wait for something, but they find it difficult to accept. Does God sometimes see us as we see our children?

Impatience may cause much greater losses than spoiled vegetable soup. We may lose the trust and respect of our children, or we may discourage others observing our lives.

When Jesus told the parable of the sower, He said, "But that on the good ground are they, which in an honest and good heart, having heard the word, keep it, and bring forth fruit with patience." If we plant an apple tree, we don't expect apples right away. We know the tree needs time to grow. As it matures, it will yield apples for us to enjoy. Likewise, our heavenly Father knows we need to mature and grow in grace and godliness. Enduring hardships produces the fruit of patience.

As we face difficult situations, we must learn to apply patience and love. These are testing times for us. We must lean on God so we can conduct ourselves as we should. God never fails to help His children when we cry out to Him. As we wait on the Lord, His joy will well up within us, and we'll find it easier to be patient. These small trials prepare us for greater tribulations we may face. Let's thank God for these opportunities to grow.

> *Dear Lord, I need your help in practicing the grace of patience. Please forgive me for my impatience with your timing in my life. In Jesus' name, Amen.*

Be still, my soul: the Lord is on thy side;
Bear patiently the cross of grief or pain;
Leave to thy God to order and provide;
In ev'ry change He faithful will remain.
Be still, my soul: thy best, thy heav'nly Friend
Through thorny ways leads to a joyful end.

—Katharina von Schlegel

Who Is Watching You?

On a mountainside in Judea one day, Jesus instructed His disciples. (See Matthew 5–7.) He taught them how to live, how to treat others, and how to withstand persecution. He taught them the necessity of keeping God's commandments. The words Christ spoke that day long ago still apply to us today.

As you go through your daily routine, know that people around you are watching your life, comparing your actions with the standard Jesus laid out in His Sermon on the Mount. Your family, a neighbor, salesman, postal worker, or cashier . . . they notice how you live. If you call yourself a Christian, you have a responsibility to live up to that name. The words you say, the things you do, the places you go, the things you listen to should befit a person dedicated to God.

As mothers, grandmothers, and single ladies, children look to us as examples. We have an important job to do—teaching and training children in the ways of God. Very likely, they will imitate what we say and do. Children can sense insincerity on our part, and they pick out our inconsistencies.

Jesus tells us, "Love your enemies, bless them that curse you, do good to them that hate you, and pray for them which despitefully use you, and persecute you" (Matthew 5:44). This runs counter to our natural urges; we can only live this way by God's grace. This kind of supernatural love will convict the sinner and perhaps convert him. Fighting back or returning evil for evil is not fitting for a child of God. Instead of resisting, we ought to turn our cheek to accept pain and to go the second mile, giving more than others demand. Remember, people watch our lives. What do they see?

Sisters, do not grow weary in loving and serving. Take fresh courage and know God is there. When the days seem long and the trials too much, look up! God looks down in love. Ask Him for what you need. He wants to supply it. He will enable you to walk in love and holiness.

Dear Lord, I ask for grace to walk daily according to your Word. Glorifying you is important to me.
In Jesus' name, Amen.

If we say that we are Christians
Then our walk and talk should be
So the world can see a difference,
Finding no hypocrisy.

Faith That Heals

Are you carrying a burden, praying God will move in the life of your loved one? Are you longing for release from pain of your own? Time drags on, and you ask, "Lord, aren't you listening? Don't you see how my heart is hurting? Don't you care?"

God does see and care, but His ways are not our ways. He works behind the scene, preparing the way for that soul to listen to the Spirit's call. We get impatient, wanting things to happen right now. Perhaps God is working on us, too, teaching us to have faith and persevere in prayer.

When Jesus healed people here on earth, He often asked first, "Do you believe?" One day a father brought his child to Jesus for healing. The disciples had failed to help this boy who was tormented by an evil spirit. Their faith was not strong enough. When the desperate father came to Jesus, he cried out in tears, "Lord, I believe; help thou mine unbelief" (Mark 9:24).

When the woman suffering from a relentless flow of blood touched the hem of Christ's robe, by faith she was healed. Why did Jesus confront and comfort her? I think He wanted her to express her faith in the Lord who healed her, to share her testimony. Hearing what God has done for others encourages and strengthens our faith. Jesus told the trembling woman, "Go in peace" (Luke 8:48).

We don't want to be like Peter that night on the sea. He started out

216

in faith to walk to Jesus on the water, but then he began to doubt. Jesus rebuked him for his lack of faith. Instead, we should ask God to increase our faith, and we can go in peace, trusting Him to answer in His time.

Dear Lord, help me to keep holding on in prayer and faith until the answer comes, trusting you know what is best. Thank you for the many prayers you have already answered. In Jesus' name, Amen.

Give me the faith which can remove
And sink the mountain to a plain;
Give me the childlike, praying love,
Which longs to build thy house again;
Thy love, let it my heart o'erpow'r
Let it my ransomed soul devour.

I would the precious time redeem,
And longer live for this alone—
To spend and to be spent for them
Who have not yet my Savior known;
Fully on these my mission prove,
And only breathe to breathe thy love.

—Charles Wesley

True Friendship

The two friends stood shoulder to shoulder facing the king. Young David had just slain the giant who defied Israel's army, and was speaking to King Saul (see 1 Samuel 18). As Prince Jonathan listened, his soul bonded with David's. He found in David a kindred spirit. David and Jonathan made a covenant, cementing their friendship and brotherhood. Jonathan gave David his own robe, sword, bow, and girdle. With these tokens of friendship, Jonathan willingly renounced his own right to the kingdom.

Jonathan proved a true friend, often warning David when his life was in danger from King Saul, even at his own peril. After King Saul and Jonathan were killed in battle, David cared for Jonathan's lame son, restoring to him the land that had been his grandfather's. King David also honored his friend's son by inviting him to eat at the royal table for the rest of his life. The effects of David and Jonathan's friendship lasted beyond death.

Like David and Jonathan, we all want friends, people who sincerely care about us even when they see us at our worst. However, relationships require nurturing. To have a friend, we must be a friend.

Jesus says, "Greater love hath no man than this, that a man lay down his life for his friends" (John 15:13). Jesus calls us His friends if we do what He commands us—to love one another. Love pursues the best interests of others, even when it costs us heavily. Jonathan gave up his right to the kingdom of Israel, and Jesus left His position as heir of heaven's splendor to become one of us. He willingly bore the weight and penalty of the sins of the whole world on the cross, proving His great love for humanity. Today Christ stands beside His Father interceding on our behalf. What a friend!

Dear Lord, thank you for being my Redeemer and my very best Friend. I know I can always depend on you. I want to be a faithful friend to you too.
In Jesus' name, Amen.

What a Friend we have in Jesus,
All our sins and griefs to bear!
What a privilege to carry
Everything to God in prayer!
O what peace we often forfeit,
O what needless pain we bear,
All because we do not carry
Everything to God in prayer!

—Joseph M. Scriven

Judging and Grudging

One day in second grade, I lined up with my classmates to leave for music class. As we waited, some girls ahead of me began whispering and giggling. Suddenly, the teacher approached, ordering those girls to follow her. Turning to me, she said, "You come too."

"But I didn't do anything!"

"Yes, I'm sure you were involved too." She ordered us to stand with our noses in a corner for fifteen minutes.

I did as I was told, but inside I fumed. "How unfair! I'm innocent!"

That evening I poured out my woes to my mother. She encouraged me to forgive the teacher for misunderstanding the situation. Then she asked something harder. "You must forgive the girls, too, for not speaking up to clear you. Remember, don't hold a grudge. Jesus wants us to forgive others."

As Christians, how do we respond when we are misunderstood or our words misconstrued? Even Jesus faced misjudgments. People called Him a rabble rouser, a winebibber, and a blasphemer. Through it all, Jesus continued to preach truth, offering eternal life to those who would believe. In love and compassion, He healed the sick, the blind, and the lame. He wept with the bereaved and blessed the little children. Being misunderstood did not distract Him from His mission. He had come to do His Father's will, teaching about the kingdom of heaven.

As we journey through this world, we also will face misunderstandings at times. Let us not become discouraged. As we place our trust in the One who understands all, our hearts rest. If we have wronged others, we must admit it and seek forgiveness. People may try to cause trouble or smear our good name, but God will give us grace. If we keep our eyes on Jesus, our perfect example, we can forgive when we are misjudged. God will strengthen us at all times. He keeps His promises!

> *Dear Lord, help me to lean on you when I am misunderstood. Help me to love those who would do me wrong. Thank you for the peace I have when I follow you.*
> *In Jesus' name, Amen.*

When you are misunderstood,
    Look up to the Savior;
He will help you to forgive,
    Returning love and favor.

Living in Peace

Bang! Bang! Bang! The furious pounding on our apartment door stopped, replaced by an angry voice. "Are those your diapers on the basement line? Come get them right away, or I'll throw them out!"

I glanced at the clock. Five o'clock in the morning.

My husband and I, along with our infant son, were living in an apartment in Cincinnati, Ohio, while my husband attended Bible college. Since we didn't own a washer or dryer, and winter was approaching, the caretakers of the apartment had told us we could hang clothes in the basement on a certain day of the week. They asked that we take them down early the next morning.

"I'm sorry we forgot them," my husband called to our neighbor. "I'll come right away."

"What a grumpy old man!" I rolled my eyes. "Why does he have to start washing at five in the morning anyway? He doesn't even have a job. And he calls himself a Christian!" We felt tempted to turn a cold shoulder toward him after that, but we remembered the command to live at peace with others as much as possible (Romans 12:18).

So we prayed for grace to not hold a grudge. We treated the man respectfully and greeted him cheerfully. Then, unexpectedly, he apologized for his anger. We told him we had already forgiven him a long time ago. He told us we were welcome to use the basement again. "I guess I don't need to start washing at five in the morning anyway. Just don't have anything else to do, and I wake up early."

As I listened, I prayed silently, *Thank you, Lord, for helping us to respond rightly. Only you could change his heart.* How good to have peace restored between us!

We need God's grace every day to live acceptably before Him. Only by Christ's power within us can we live in peace with others, one aspect of being salt and light in this world. Our lives may be the only Bible some people read.

Dear Lord, help me to be a peacemaker, living always to glorify you. In Jesus' name, Amen.

Jesus, My Saviour

Let the envenomed heart and tongue,
The hand outstretched to do me wrong,
Excite no feelings in my breast
But such as Jesus once expressed.

To others let me always give
What I from others would receive;
Good deeds for evil ones return,
Nor, when provoked, with anger burn.

This will proclaim how bright and fair
The precepts of the Gospel are;
And God Himself, the God of love,
His own resemblance will approve.[m]

—Benjamin Beddome

[m] "Jesus, My Saviour," *The Christian Hymnary,* #292, vv. 3–5.

Instruments for God's Glory

Back in the 1960s when I was working as a nurse's aide in the hospital, I took care of setting up the delivery room before a birth. After a delivery, I washed the used instruments, wrapped them in towels, taped them shut, and placed them in an instrument called an autoclave. This heated the instruments to sterilize them. When they had cooled, I placed them in their proper places in the delivery room, which I had also cleaned thoroughly. The room and its contents stood ready for use.

These instruments played a part in the safe delivery of a precious baby. Their usefulness, however, depended on their being sanitized and stored in their proper places. Similarly, God can only use us when we have been washed in Christ's blood and made pure. We also need to remain in the place where God wants us. As part of His church, His willing instruments, we bring glory to Him.

Some of the instruments in the delivery room had the potential to be used for evil purposes, but in this case they were used to help a mother and her baby. As Romans 6:13 puts it, "Neither yield ye your members as instruments of unrighteousness unto sin: but yield yourselves unto God, as those that are alive from the dead, and your members as instruments of righteousness unto God."

Are we using our hands, feet, minds, and voices to glorify God? Are we asking Christ for protection and power to resist sin? Will we serve as tools for Satan or tools Christ can use in His kingdom work? The Apostle Paul tells us that if we offer ourselves as slaves to righteousness, leading to holiness, God will reward us with eternal life (Romans 6:19–22).

The instruments I prepared were inanimate; they did not resist, no matter what I did to them. However, we have the power of choice. We often resist the purging and heat that prepare us for usefulness in God's work. Are we willing to serve quietly without recognition? Can we yield ourselves as willing instruments, submissive and pliable in God's hands for His glory?

> *Dear Lord, use me for your glory in whatever way you wish. I am so grateful for all you have done for me. In Jesus' name, Amen.*

To serve you in your kingdom, Lord,
 Is what I want to do;
An instrument which you can use
 To help a soul to you.

Waiting on the Lord

No one enjoys waiting, whether at a traffic light or in a doctor's office. Our society expects immediate gratification—instant mashed potatoes, one-hour photos, and kiosk orders at fast food restaurants.

Yet we women often find ourselves in a season of waiting. Single women struggle, wondering, "Will I ever have a husband? Will I have to go through life alone?" Married women who long for children ask, "When will I bear a child?" Some mothers wonder when God will answer their prayers for a wayward child. Other women with adult children wait longingly for grandchildren. God often asks us to wait for an answer to our prayers, to trust and believe in Him, and to hope.

Waiting is hard. We feel like nothing is happening, and we want an answer now. So what can we do while we wait? The prophet Jeremiah describes moments of deep despair as he endured calamities and suffered for his faithfulness to God (see Lamentations 3). His discouragement lifted when he recognized God's faithfulness and decided to trust God and wait for His deliverance (vv. 18–26). Later in the same passage, Jeremiah paints a word picture of full surrender to God—lifting up his heart with his hands, offering it to God (v. 41).

The psalmist David told God, "On thee do I wait all the day" (Psalm 25:5). While he waited, he asked God to teach him His ways and lead him in the truth. He recalled God's tender mercies and loving kindnesses in the past, and he pled for God's mercy (v. 6).

Do you ever find yourself like Jeremiah, discouraged because your prayers go unanswered? You question and struggle, but God still says, "Wait." Instead of giving up hope, take heed to David's advice: "Wait on the LORD: be of good courage, and he shall strengthen thine heart: wait, I say, on the LORD" (Psalm 27:14). One day all waiting will come to an end, and God's children will experience the fulfillment of every holy desire in His presence.

Dear Lord, help me to trust you when I have to wait, to believe you hear and will answer in your time and way. Thank you for your faithfulness. In Jesus' name, Amen.

Wait on God, and trust Him through all thy days;
Cast thy cares upon Him who guides all thy ways.
Do not despair; as the morning fair
Scatters fog and darkness, God removes thy care.
'Midst all thy trials, in all thy care
God remains thy faithful Friend everywhere.

—Johann Friedrich Rader[n]

[n] *The Christian Hymnary*, #305.

Contentment

Ladies, try comparing the amount of luggage we carry on a trip with the amount a man needs. Quite a difference! Yet many of our items seem essential. In our housekeeping we face the same problem; we accumulate stuff until we reach the point of needing to have a garage sale.

Both men and women desire possessions. Some people even worry about what will happen to their belongings when they die. Will their things receive proper care, or will they be sold to a stranger?

Though our possessions may not be evil in themselves, our attachment to them can be wrong. God always wants our first love. The above Scripture reading gives us the right perspective. Realizing we can't take anything with us when we die, why do we wear ourselves out to gain temporal things? Do we think they will satisfy us? We ought to content ourselves with the basic necessities—food and clothing (1 Timothy 6:8). Being content means we are satisfied, peaceful, and happy. True contentment comes only when we have surrendered ourselves and our possessions to Christ. As we stay close to God, the lure of riches loses its hold on us.

God knows that even if we owned all the world's riches, we would still long for more. Seeking the things of this world only brings leanness to our souls and dissatisfaction to our hearts. Instead, let us find contentment in Jesus Christ, the source of all true joys. He offers all we need and more.

Sister, are you filling your heart and life with perishable things, or are you laying up treasures in heaven (Matthew 6:20)? Do you trust in uncertain riches, or in the living God who gives us richly all things to enjoy (1 Timothy 6:17)?

Finding fulfillment in Christ makes it easier to see the needs of others—the poor, sick, lonely, and the millions who don't know Christ or even have His Word. How blessed we are to know Jesus as our all in all! Will we draw closer to God, allowing the things of this world to lose their hold on us? If so, we will find freedom to serve God in ways we never imagined.

Dear Lord, I desire to be a godly woman for your glory, seeking the contentment only you can give. Help me to keep you as my first love. In Jesus' name, Amen.

Contentment! O how sweet
 To trust in God each day,
To know He cares for me
 And hears me when I pray.

Bigger and Better

Many people get sucked into the current of bigger and better. Some buy a huge flat-screen television even though it barely fits into their living room. Others purchase a new car just because their neighbor did.

Can we Christians get caught up in this current too? It can easily happen if we relax our guard. Perhaps our kitchen functions well, but looks out of style. We feel the pressure to update it. After all, our friends are doing it, why can't we? Before making a decision like this, let's check our motives—and our budget.

The problem of wanting to keep up with our peers or trying to outdo others has plagued humanity throughout history. Do we see this trend in ourselves? Do we wish to excel in something because we yearn to exceed the abilities of others? Do we want to get a new dress every time our friends do or plan a fantastic vacation because someone else did? If we do, we must take inventory of our hearts. Instead of pursuing bigger and better, Jesus urges, "Take my yoke upon you, and learn of me; for I am meek and lowly in heart: and ye shall find rest unto your souls" (Matthew 11:29). If we hand in our resignation to self—a relentless taskmaster—Christ will give us contented hearts and rest in our souls.

Meekness adds beauty to our souls. The psalmist writes, "He will beautify the meek with salvation" (Psalm 149:4). Meekness ranks among the fruit of the Spirit (Galatians 5:22–23), and the Apostle

Paul expands this theme in Philippians 2:3: "Let nothing be done through strife or vainglory; but in lowliness of mind let each esteem other better than themselves." What do others observe in your life? Do they see pride or a meek and quiet spirit (1 Peter 3:4)? Don't get snared in the trap of wanting to outdo others. Rather, focus on pleasing your heavenly Father. Meekness is priceless in His sight.

Dear Lord, I ask you to give me a meek and lowly heart.
I desire to be a godly, chaste woman.
In Jesus' name, Amen.

Forgive me, Lord, for coveting
    The paltry things of earth;
But rather, help me seek each day
    The things of greater worth.

Showing Hospitality

"Company's coming!" Does the thought bring us joy or anxiety? The Apostle Paul lists "given to hospitality" as a quality we ought to develop (Romans 12:13). In His poignant description of the final judgment, Jesus emphasizes hospitality: "For I was an hungred, and ye gave me meat: I was thirsty, and ye gave me drink: I was a stranger, and ye took me in: naked, and ye clothed me" (Matthew 25:35–36). How would our actions change if we treated each guest in our home or each visitor in our church as we would treat Jesus?

Although Jesus had no place to call His home, the Gospels record accounts of Him showing hospitality (Matthew 14:15–21; 15:29–38). He had been teaching the people, and they had followed Him into the wilderness. As evening approached, the disciples asked Jesus to send the people away to buy food, but Jesus told His disciples to feed them. From a boy's small lunch a company of thousands received sustenance. Big baskets of leftovers stood as evidence of the heavenly Father's bounty. Jesus had met their needs, both physical and spiritual. Does He not call His followers to do the same?

A good hostess puts her guests at ease, making them feel at home. Her house doesn't need the latest décor or meticulous cleaning. Her menu need not be elaborate. She should take a lesson from the story of Mary and Martha (Luke 10:38–42). Martha worked herself into a stew trying to care for her guests. Meanwhile, Mary sat at Jesus' feet, drinking in His words. When Martha complained to Jesus about her shirking sister, Jesus rebuked her for her preoccupation with material things. If Martha had laid aside her pride, perhaps she, too, could have found time to sit at Jesus' feet.

Hospitality extends to our neighbors. How do we feel about the neighbor who often borrows a cup of this or that? Do the interruptions to our routine irritate us? Our time and possessions really belong to God, not to us. Do we miss opportunities to share the Gospel with others because of our selfishness?

Strive to live as Christ's representative, and serve your guests as graciously and courteously as you would serve Christ. You have succeeded as a hostess if your guests see Christ in you.

> *Dear Lord, help me to put important things first, serving others as I would serve you. In Jesus' name, Amen.*

O man redeemed, fold to thy heart thy brother;
Where love prevails, the peace of God is there;
To worship rightly and to love each other
Makes life a hymn, each kindly deed a prayer.

For he whom Jesus loved hath truly spoken;
Love's greater service which He deigns to bless
Restores the lost, and binds the spirit broken,
And feeds the widow and the fatherless.°

—John G. Whittier

° *The Christian Hymnary,* #430.

The Joy of Giving

Are you a giver or a taker? Do you find it a joy to give your money, time, or possessions? A willing, generous heart pleases our heavenly Father.

In today's reading Paul encouraged the Corinthians to emulate the churches of Macedonia who had excelled in the grace of giving. Although those in Macedonia were facing afflictions and tribulations, and experiencing great poverty as well, they had outdone themselves in giving alms for the support and relief of the Jerusalem Christians. As we see a need, we too should open our hands, giving liberally.

When self is laid on the altar, it is not difficult to lay our pocketbooks there, too. Realizing we are not our own, but God's, and all we call our own is His, helps us to give as God gives. His liberality is seen in all the blessings He showers on his people. Even those who do not acknowledge him as Lord are recipients of God's grace.

We've probably all heard the expression, "We can't out-give God." When we have given as the Lord desires us to give, we will be blessed, whether in financial return, or in spiritual blessings of greater worth.

However, if we put our money in the church offering while wishing we could have kept it and spent it on ourselves, we will receive no blessing. In 2 Corinthians 9:7 we see God doesn't want us to give grudgingly, but He loves a cheerful giver. Giving with a bountiful hand blesses not only those who receive, but also the giver. The recipients often pray for the giver, and they, too, are inspired to give to others in whatever way they can. Giving from the heart begins a cycle—someday we may be the grateful receiver rather than the generous giver.

We who are blessed with material things should never forget that Christ left untold riches to become poor, so we could become rich. How can we withhold our hand from those who are in need? When we give as unto the Lord, we will be filled with joy.

Dear Lord, thank you for giving all for me. May my heart be willing to give liberally and cheerfully, remembering that all I have is yours. In Jesus' name, Amen.

O seek to honor God
    With a heart grateful and true;
Remember God's own gift:
    He sent His Son to you.

Unclasp your hand and give;
    With joy an offering bring;
The Lord will surely bless,
    And cause your heart to sing.

God's Eye Is on the Widow

In the Old Testament God gave strict instructions to ensure care for widows. The Israelites were required to leave some of their sheaves, olives, and grapes for widows and other poor people to glean (Deuteronomy 24:19–22). God also commanded His people to share part of their tithe with needy people. God said, "Ye shall not afflict any widow, or fatherless child. If thou afflict them in any wise, and they cry at all unto me, I will surely hear their cry" (Exodus 22:22–23). God's eye watches over the helpless. The prophet Isaiah pronounced woes on those who preyed upon the widows and the fatherless (Isaiah 10:1–2).

The Gospel of Luke records an account of Christ's compassion for a widow in dire straits (7:11–16). Her only son had died. Christ stopped the procession carrying the bier and raised the son to life.

New Testament believers continued the tradition of the church caring for her widows. Visiting and helping widows ranks high on God's list of priorities: "Pure religion and undefiled before God and the Father is this, to visit the fatherless and widows in their affliction, and to keep himself unspotted from the world" (James 1:27).

If you are a widow, know that God cares for you. You may not find yourself at the brink of starvation as did the widow of Zarephath (1 Kings 17:9–12). Whatever needs you have, however, God sees them and He cares. Cry out to God and tell Him your needs. God will sustain you through your darkest hours. Although God's words in Isaiah 54:5 also apply to Christ's bride, the church, claim this promise as your own: "Thy Maker is thine husband." God will never desert you.

Dear Lord, help me to have compassion for others, treating them as I would want to be treated. Show me how I can be an encouragement to widows and others who are alone. In Jesus' name, Amen.

Although your heart is breaking,
    And you feel so all alone,
Cry out to God! He hears you,
    And His heart is not as stone.
The Lord is your true comfort
    For He holds you in His hand;
He sees your tears, and whispers,
    "Dear child, I understand."

An Evening Song

At dusk a bird outside my window sings his evening song. Even when it's raining, I hear his joyful trills, and the song speaks to me. In the quietness of the evening, where do my thoughts turn? Do I praise God for His presence with me? Nothing that transpires throughout the little bird's day lessens his desire to sing. He does what God intends him to do.

Evening provides the chance to reflect on my day. Did I use my time wisely? Did my tongue speak only kindness? Did I use good judgment? Before I lie down at night, I want to right any wrongs I may have done. If I spoke harshly to someone, I need to ask forgiveness. If I was offended by someone's words, I need to lay it down. I never want to carry grudges overnight. Clear, open relationships with God and with others afford me the best sleep aid available.

Reflecting on the blessings of the day not only helps our perspective, but also causes praise to well up from our souls. What a marvel that God cares about us! Psalm 104 describes the way God cares for and sustains His creation. As the psalmist contemplated these things, he said, "I will sing unto the LORD as long as I live: I will sing praise to my God while I have my being. My meditation of him shall be sweet: I will be glad in the LORD" (vv. 33–34).

Take time in the evening to count the day's blessings. Encourage your children or grandchildren to do the same. Look for the small, unnoticed joys in life. Thank God for the small arms that reach up to you, for the laughter of little girls, for the busy boys who can't seem to sit still, for the teens who need a listening ear. Appreciate the season of life that provides more quiet and leisure time as you age. Every phase of life contains its set of blessings. Do you appreciate them? God is good. He loads us with benefits (Psalm 68:19). Offer Him an evening song of praise.

Dear Lord, I want to offer you a song of praise, for you are worthy. Help me to be more grateful, counting my blessings every day. In Jesus' name, Amen.

Evening Prayer

If I have wounded any soul today,
If I have caused one foot to go astray,
If I have walked in my own willful way,
Dear Lord, forgive!

If I have been perverse, or hard, or cold,
If I have longed for shelter in Thy fold,
When thou hast given me some fort to hold,
Dear Lord, forgive!

—C. Maude Battersby

Christ, Our Anchor

Suicide. Such a tragedy. I had just heard news of someone who felt he could not face life anymore. Everyday living seemed too difficult, the future too frightening. Distrust, fear, loneliness, unhappiness, grief, despair, and defeat had filled that person's mind until all hope had vanished.

How different the outlook of us who believe! In Christ, we have hope. Today's reading describes that hope as the anchor of our soul, steadfast and sure (v. 19). As our High Priest, Christ hears our prayers and intercedes for us (v. 20). We don't need to face the storms alone, adrift on the sea of life to fend for ourselves. Christ is both our guide and anchor. Whether day or night, He hears our prayers.

The patriarch Abraham left home and country, not knowing where God would lead him (Genesis 12:1–4). He endured struggles and hardships on the way and stumbled a few times, yet he remained faithful to God. God never promises His children an easy life, but He asks us to trust Him and to anchor in His promises.

Can we give God our fears and insecurities, our today and tomorrows? Christ wants to give us His peace, His joy, and His love. He fills our emptiness and drives away our doubt and despair. He offers us hope, not just for today, but for the future.

Rewards await those who endure: "Blessed is the man that endureth temptation: for when he is tried, he shall receive the crown of life, which the Lord hath promised to them that love him" (James 1:12). "Now the God of hope fill you with all joy and peace in believing, that ye may abound in hope, through the power of the Holy Ghost" (Romans 15:13).

Persevere, dear friend! You can trust the anchor of your soul with your future.

> *Dear Lord, I put my trust and hope in you, giving you my fears, and anticipating the future when I will be with you eternally. Help me to be faithful.*
> *In Jesus' name, Amen.*

Not a shadow can rise,

Not a cloud in the skies,

But His smile quickly drives it away;

Not a doubt nor a fear,

Not a sigh nor a tear,

Can abide while we trust and obey.[p]

—John H. Sammis

---

[p] "Trust and Obey," *Christian Hymnal* #465, v. 2.

What Is Your Score?

I still remember the feeling of tension in the room as my classmates and I sweated through achievement tests. These tests revealed what we had attained academically, and we wanted to do our best.

How do we grade our spiritual achievement? Can we or others see our knowledge of God's Word growing and our daily walk with the Lord progressing? The Apostle Paul encouraged the believers at Colosse by telling them of his joy in hearing they were walking in Christ and were steadfast in the faith which they had been taught (Colossians 2:5–7). How do we score?

When the top students in the local school were sent to take state achievement tests, teachers encouraged them to do their best and make their school proud of them. The Apostle Paul also must have felt pleasure in seeing the progress of those whom he had taught: "For what is our hope, or joy, or crown of rejoicing? Are not even ye in the presence of our Lord Jesus Christ at his coming? For ye are our glory and joy" (1 Thessalonians 2:19–20).

So how can we do our best in our Christian life?

We need the Lord's strength to overcome the temptations we encounter. Ephesians 6:10–18 describes the armor that enables us to win the battle over sin and have victory in our walk with God. This consists of the belt of truth, the breastplate of righteousness, the Gospel of peace for our feet, the shield of faith to withstand Satan's darts, the helmet of salvation, and the sword of the Spirit. We are to cover ourselves with prayer at all times and remain alert to the dangers around us.

Christ wants us to stand strong so He can present us to the Father as "holy and unblameable and unreproveable in his sight" (Colossians 1:22). As 2 Timothy 2:15 says, "Study to show thyself approved unto God, a workman that needeth not to be ashamed, rightly dividing the word of truth." Only the students with top scores received certificates of award in school, but with the Lord's help we can all win the highest honor—eternal life.

Dear Lord, thank you for going before us. Help me to use the weapons and protections you offer so I can do my best, in your strength, to grow in faith. In Jesus' name, Amen.

Be faithful to the end!
Let not danger nor distress
Make thy heart love Jesus less.
Until death trust thou that Friend!
Ah! the suffering of this earth,
All the glory is not worth
Which thy Lord will give to thee
When up yonder thou shalt be.

—Anna Bartlett Warner

The Angels Rejoice

One of my older cousins did not have long to live. Soft-spoken and kind, she was beloved by all, but she had never yielded to Christ. As I approached her bed, I saw her familiar smile and twinkling eyes. She reached eagerly for my hands. After we had greeted each other, she asked, "Did you know I belong to Jesus now? I am so happy!"

Soon after she had become ill, her son—a minister—had sensed her fear of death. He spoke to her of Jesus and how He died so we could live forever. With tears, she asked her son, "Will Jesus forgive me after all these years I have refused Him?"

"Yes, Mom, He loves you and is calling you to come." She found Jesus that day.

Tears of joy flowed as we talked, and I knew she had become a different person. She could scarcely wait to see Jesus. She spoke to every person who visited her, encouraging all to believe in Christ and be ready to face death. Although her death was imminent, I knew I would see her again in heaven.

Following His parable of the lost sheep, Jesus says, "There is joy in the presence of the angels of God over one sinner that repenteth" (Luke 15:10). I knew the angels were rejoicing over my cousin. She would soon be home.

Not long ago, a friend was headed out the door to go on an errand when she collapsed. She had suffered a massive heart attack and died on the spot. She had no warning, no time to say goodbye, no time to pray. We rejoiced that she was ready to go, prepared to meet her Savior. But how many others are not prepared?

Today we each need to take stock of our lives. Are we ready? Are we at peace with everyone? Have we done what we could to share the Gospel with others? Have we prayed for lost souls? Are we walking in obedience to Christ in all things? We might have only today, perhaps only this hour or moment. When death calls, we must go.

Death is so final. But for those who belong to Jesus, death opens the door to fullness of life.

Have the angels rejoiced at your repentance? Will they welcome you into the eternal home one day? If something stands between you and Christ, then make it right. If you are walking with Jesus in repentance and holiness, your hope extends beyond the grave.

Dear Lord, thank you for hope beyond the grave. Help me to be faithful every day so I am ready for your call, "Come home!" In Jesus' name, Amen.

Ready to speak, ready to warn,
Ready o'er souls to yearn;
Ready in life, ready in death,
Ready for His return.

—A. C. Palmer[q]

q "Ready to Suffer," *The Christian Hymnary* #368, v. 4.

A Holy Calling

L. E. Maxwell said, "We have been destined for a crown only if we choose the cross."[22] The Apostle Paul told the church at Thessalonica he was blessed to hear of their patience and faith as they endured hardship, reminding them that their faith under fire would glorify God (2 Thessalonians 1:4–5, 12). We have a holy calling—to stand for Christ, to bear affliction for His cause and His glory. We cannot do this in our own strength, for our strength lies only in Christ. In the face of doubts and fears, our trust leans on our mighty God. Even if men take our lives, our hope goes on, for it resides in Jesus. We shall receive the crown of life!

The Apostle James encourages the saints, telling them to be patient and to endure (James 5:7–10). He reminds them of the prophets who suffered for speaking the truth. They serve as examples for us of faithfulness and patience. He continues, "Behold, we count them happy which endure" (v. 11). The Apostle Paul exhorts Timothy, "Thou therefore endure hardness, as a good soldier of Jesus Christ," (2 Timothy 2:3).

Hardship ought not to surprise us. "Yea, and all that will live godly in Christ Jesus shall suffer persecution," Paul tells Timothy (2 Timothy 3:12). Peter tells believers to not be surprised when they suffer a fiery trial, as though it were some strange thing happening, but to rejoice! When we are partakers of Christ's sufferings, we will have exceeding joy when His glory is revealed (1 Peter 4:12–13).

Are we daily choosing to follow Christ, even when it means we must suffer rather than deny our Lord? If so, we are aligning ourselves with faithful ones who have gone before, and will share in the glory of our risen Lord!

Dear Lord, help me to be true to you in every situation. Help me focus on the future you have in store for the faithful believer and not on what I may suffer here. In Jesus' name, Amen.

Go, then, earthly fame and treasure!
Come, disaster, scorn, and pain!
In thy service, pain is pleasure,
With thy favor, loss is gain!
I have called thee Abba, Father!
I have stayed my heart on thee.
Storms may howl, and clouds may gather,
All must work for good to me.

Man may trouble and distress me,
'Twill but drive me to thy breast;
Life with trials hard may press me;
Heav'n will bring me sweeter rest.
O 'tis not in grief to harm me,
While thy love is left to me;
O 'twere not in joy to charm me,
Were that joy unmixed with thee.

—Henry F. Lyte[r]

[r] "Jesus, I My Cross Have Taken," *Hymns of the Church*, #540, vv. 2 and 3.

Bound by Sin

I gazed out the window at the snow-covered yard, glistening in the sunlight as though covered with an icy sheen. The road will be treacherous, *I thought idly.*

As I watched, someone came swiftly down the hill on a sled. Fearing they were going too fast to make the sharp bend in the road just past our house, I ran outside, hoping to warn the sled rider of the peril ahead. If he could not make the curve, he would fall to the dangerous rocks below.

Running as swiftly as I could, I called out, "Stop! Danger ahead!" Before I could grasp him, he passed beyond my reach. Even as I heard his cry of terror, I turned and saw another sled approaching. Desperately I grabbed at this sled, pulling it off the road to safety. Then another sled came into view! I rescued this one too. Again and again, I snagged the sled riders as they came near me. Finally I felt so exhausted. I wanted to run for help, but if I did, how many would be lost while I was gone?

I began to notice a strange thing about the sled riders. How horrible! They were chained or tied onto the sleds in such a way that they could not free themselves. I continued to pull as many as I could from the slippery slope, but I could not save them all. I wept as I worked, and my strength gradually ebbed.

When I awoke from this dream, I was crying. I prayed, "O Lord, what does this dream mean?" I believe I was watching souls bound by Satan's chains going headlong down the treacherous slope of sin, heedless of the danger ahead and helpless to break sin's bondage.

As believers, we must warn souls of the danger ahead, persuading them that Christ alone can break their chains of sin and set them free. May we be alert and seek out the lost sheep and bring them in.

Jesus says, "Ye shall know the truth, and the truth shall make you free" (John 8:32). Are we sharing this truth with others? Christ can set people free!

Thank you, Lord, for setting me free. Help me to warn those still bound by sin and show them the way to true liberty in you. In Jesus' name, Amen.

T'ward hell you hasten in conceit,

You plunge in sin's perdition;

Yet wisdom cries upon the street,

In God there is redemption.

—Daniel S. Warner

249

Till the Dawn

Some nights I have trouble sleeping. Dawn seems to creep in on leaden feet. But someday another dawn is coming when Christ will return for His children. Reading the daily news reminds me how heavily the darkness presses around us. I wonder, "How much worse can it get? What lies ahead for our children and grandchildren?" In a world gone mad, where violence appears to go unchecked, the future indeed looks bleak.

Satan laughs as he sees society, and even churches, falling for his lies. People flaunt their freedom to live however they wish, promoting behaviors that God condemns. Christians are accused of hate speech when they stand for the right. What a topsy-turvy world!

Are we yearning for Christ's return? As the darkness becomes more oppressive, we must set our focus on the Lord. In times like these, we ought to heed this counsel: "Ponder the path of thy feet, and let all thy ways be established. Turn not to the right hand nor to the left: remove thy foot from evil" (Proverbs 4:26–27).

Although wickedness permeates the world and sometimes churches, we have a path, shining with the light of Christ, in which to walk. Let us keep pressing on till the dawn breaks and we see Jesus. God has not left us desolate!

We must fill our hearts and minds with God's Word and fervently pray for our families and others. We need to use our time wisely by reaching out to the lost, and not allow fear to dictate our actions. One day Christ will return—O glorious daybreak! He will right all wrongs, and we shall be like Him, for we shall see Him as He is. We shall be with Him forever where night will never come. Let us keep growing into His likeness, dear ones. We will soon see Jesus!

Dear Lord, I thank you that I can trust in you in this scary world. Help me to stay on your shining path and not fear the future. In Jesus' name, Amen.

Hold on till the daybreak;
O what joy we'll know
When Christ in His glory
Returns for His own!

Index to Scripture Readings

Genesis 2:18–25 130

Genesis 3:1–12.. 16

Deuteronomy 6:4–9 138

2 Samuel 12:1–14 20

1 Kings 3:16–27 178

1 Kings 17:1–16 236

1 Chronicles 29:9–17. 38

Psalm 9:1–10 174

Psalm 14 74

Psalm 17:1–9 96

Psalm 29:1–11 88

Psalm 31 98

Psalm 34:8 22

Psalm 36:5–12 86

Psalm 51:10–17 50

Psalm 66:8–20 204

Psalm 89:1–18 104

Psalm 91 100

Psalm 92 206

Psalm 95:1–9 32

Psalm 99 90

Psalm 105:1–7 208

Psalm 113 238

Psalm 118:1–14 82

Psalm 119:97–112 22

Psalm 119:129–136 28

Psalm 119:145–160 66

Psalm 130 226

Psalm 139:1–12, 23–24 198

Psalm 142:1–7 80

Psalm 143 46

Psalm 146 194

Psalm 148 40

Proverbs 2:1–9 188

Proverbs 12:15–28 192

Proverbs 7:1–5 146

Proverbs 31:10–31 . . . . . .132, 150

Ecclesiastes 5:10–20 64

Isaiah 12 42

Isaiah 43:1–11 184

Daniel 4:29–37. 166

Matthew 5:33–48. 214

Matthew 6:5–15 . . . . .44, 168

Matthew 7:21–29. . . . . . .30, 162

Matthew 11:28–30 26

Matthew 16:24–28 112

Matthew 20:20–28 202

Matthew 25:1–13 122

Mark 10:2–12 140

Mark 14:26–42 124

Luke 6:27–38 220

Luke 7:36–50 232

Luke 8:43–48 216

Luke 11:34–44 126

Luke 12:15–26 230

Luke 12:27–34 70

Luke 14:25–33 110

Luke 15:1–10 244

Luke 15:11–24 176

Luke 16:10–13 36

Luke 16:19–31 84

Luke 18:9–14 186

Luke 24:13–53 60

John 3:14–21 14

John 4:5–24 144

John 14:15–23 24

John 15:1–13 58

John 19:1–19 102

Romans 6:16–23 .. ..106, 248

Romans 8:31–39 120

Romans 9:15–21 114

Romans 12:1–13 224

Romans 12:17–21 222

1 Corinthians 12:12–20 68

1 Corinthians 13 164

2 Corinthians 8:1–15 234

Ephesians 3:8–21 200

Ephesians 4:17–32 .. .. ..134, 196

Ephesians 5:1–8 148

Ephesians 5:8–14 152

Ephesians 5:15–21 154

Ephesians 6:10–20 118

Philippians 2:5–8 26

Colossians 3:1–17 48

Colossians 3:18–24 158

1 Thessalonians 3:12–13 160

1 Thessalonians 4:13–18 .. 56, 160

2 Thessalonians 1:1–12 .. 116, 246

1 Timothy 6:6–19 .. .. .. .34, 228

2 Timothy 2:20–26 190

2 Timothy 3:1–12 250

2 Timothy 3:10–17 242

Titus 2:1–15 210

Titus 2:3–5 158

Hebrews 4 128

Hebrews 6:9–20 240

Hebrews 11:23–40 180

Hebrews 12:5–11 54

James 1 62

James 3 170

James 4:4–10 72

James 5:13–20 92

1 Peter 1:1–21 94

1 Peter 3:1–11 .. ..156, 172

1 Peter 4:12–19 108

2 Peter 1:1–11 .. ..136, 212

2 Peter 3:9–14 52

1 John 1:1–10 18

1 John 2:15–17 182

1 John 3:10–18 218

1 John 4:7–11 142

Revelation 20:11–15 78

Revelation 21:1–10 76

Endnotes

[1] Richard J. Foster, *Celebration of Discipline: The Path to Spiritual Growth*, Harper & Row, San Francisco, 1988, p. 111.

[2] C. S. Lewis, *Reflections on the Psalms*, Harcourt, Brace & Co., New York, 1958, pp. 93–97.

[3] Matthew Henry, *Matthew Henry Commentary on the Whole Bible (Complete)*, <https://www.biblestudytools.com/commentaries/matthew-henry-complete/psalms/149.html>, accessed on June 24, 2019.

[4] "Spider," *Wikipedia, The Free Encyclopedia*, <https://en.wikipedia.org/w/index.php?title=Spider&oldid=862278307>, accessed on June 24, 2019.

[5] Charles Wesley, "Thy Ceaseless, Unexhausted Love," Hymnary.org, <https://hymnary.org/text/thy_ceaseless_unexhausted_love>, accessed on June 24, 2019.

[6] *The Authorized King James Bible*, Cambridge University Press, p. 5.

[7] Arthur S. Maxwell, *Uncle Arthur's Bedtime Stories*, Review and Herald Publishing Assoc., Hagerstown, MD, 1966. Vol. 13, pp. 9–13.

[8] Marshall Broomhall, M.A., *Hudson Taylor, the Man Who Believed God*, R. R. Clark, Limited, Edinburgh, Great Britain, 1929, p. 144.

[9] Ibid., p. 201.

[10] Ibid., p. 219.

[11] L. E. Maxwell, *Born Crucified,* Moody Bible Institute of Chicago, 1945, p.180

[12] Broomhall, p. 173.

[13] L. E. Maxwell, p. 190.

[14] Stephen Grellet, goodreads.com, <https://www.goodreads.com/quotes/131923-i-shall-pass-through-this-world-but-once-any-good>, accessed on July 1, 2019.

[15] Elisabeth Elliot, *Let Me Be a Woman,* Tyndale House Publishers, Wheaton, IL, 1976, back cover.

[16] Margaret D. Nadauld, goodreads.com, <https://www.goodreads.com/quotes/295107-women-of-god-can-never-be-like-women-of-the>, accessed on July 1, 2019.

[17] Jasmine Cruz, "Marriage Takes Three," Poetry Soup, 2014, <https://www.poetrysoup.com/poem/marriage_takes_three_614680>, accessed on July 1, 2019.

[18] Christina Georgina Rossetti, "O Christ Our All in Each, Our All in All," <https://www.poetrynook.com/poem/o-christ-our-all-each-our-all-all>, accessed December 13, 2018.

[19] Broomhall, p. 20.

[20] Max Hunter Folk Song Collection, <https://maxhunter.missouristate.edu/songinformation.aspx?ID=99>, accessed on July 8, 2019.

[21] "Frances Jane van Alystyne (Fanny Crosby)," Faith Hall of Fame, <http://eaec.org/faithhallfame/fanny_crosby.htm>, accessed July 8, 2019.

[22] L. E. Maxwell, p. 177.

About the Author

Wilma Webb lives with her husband Lloyd near Spencerville, Indiana. In over fifty years of marriage, they have been blessed with seven children, twenty-six grandchildren, and two great-grandchildren. Wilma enjoys writing not only devotionals and poetry but also songs. After her children were grown, she took up painting as a hobby. Wilma is the author of *Words for Women,* also published by Christian Aid Ministries.

Wilma is a member of Hicksville Christian Fellowship in northwestern Ohio. She enjoys hearing from readers. You may email her at wilmawebb46@live.com or write to her in care of Christian Aid Ministries, P. O. Box 360, Berlin, OH 44610.

About Christian Aid Ministries

Christian Aid Ministries was founded in 1981 as a nonprofit, tax-exempt 501(c)(3) organization. Its primary purpose is to provide a trustworthy and efficient channel for Amish, Mennonite, and other conservative Anabaptist groups and individuals to minister to physical and spiritual needs around the world. This is in response to the command to ". . . do good unto all men, especially unto them who are of the household of faith" (Galatians 6:10).

Each year, CAM supporters provide 15–20 million pounds of food, clothing, medicines, seeds, Bibles, Bible story books, and other Christian literature for needy people. Most of the aid goes to orphans and Christian families. Supporters' funds also help to clean up and rebuild for natural disaster victims, put up Gospel billboards in the U.S., support several church-planting efforts, operate two medical clinics, and provide resources for needy families to make their own living. CAM's main purposes for providing aid are to help and encourage God's people and bring the Gospel to a lost and dying world.

CAM has staff, warehouses, and distribution networks in Romania, Moldova, Ukraine, Haiti, Nicaragua, Liberia, Israel, and Kenya. Aside from management, supervisory personnel, and bookkeeping operations, volunteers do most of the work at CAM locations. Each year, volunteers at our warehouses, field bases, Disaster Response Services projects, and other locations donate over 200,000 hours of work.

CAM's ultimate purpose is to glorify God and help enlarge His kingdom. ". . . whatsoever ye do, do all to the glory of God" (1 Corinthians 10:31).

The Way to God and Peace

We live in a world contaminated by sin. Sin is anything that goes against God's holy standards. When we do not follow the guidelines that God our Creator gave us, we are guilty of sin. Sin separates us from God, the source of life.

Since the time when the first man and woman, Adam and Eve, sinned in the Garden of Eden, sin has been universal. The Bible says that we all have "sinned and come short of the glory of God" (Romans 3:23). It also says that the natural consequence for that sin is eternal death, or punishment in an eternal hell: "Then when lust hath conceived, it bringeth forth sin: and sin, when it is finished, bringeth forth death" (James 1:15).

But we do not have to suffer eternal death in hell. God provided forgiveness for our sins through the death of His only Son, Jesus Christ. Because Jesus was perfect and without sin, He could die in our place. "For God so loved the world that he gave his only begotten Son, that whosoever believeth in him should not perish, but have everlasting life" (John 3:16).

A sacrifice is something given to benefit someone else. It costs the giver greatly. Jesus was God's sacrifice. Jesus' death takes away the penalty of sin for all those who accept this sacrifice and truly repent of their sins.

To repent of sins means to be truly sorry for and turn away from the things we have done that have violated God's standards (Acts 2:38; 3:19).

Jesus died, but He did not remain dead. After three days, God's Spirit miraculously raised Him to life again. God's Spirit does something similar in us. When we receive Jesus as our sacrifice and repent of our sins, our hearts are changed. We become spiritually alive! We develop new desires and attitudes (2 Corinthians 5:17). We begin to make choices that please God (1 John 3:9). If we do fail and commit sins, we can ask God for forgiveness. "If we confess our sins, he is faithful and just to forgive us our sins, and to cleanse us from all unrighteousness" (1 John 1:9).

Once our hearts have been changed, we want to continue growing spiritually. We will be happy to let Jesus be the Master of our lives and will want to become more like Him. To do this, we must meditate on God's Word and commune with God in prayer. We will testify to others of this change by being baptized and sharing the good news of God's victory over sin and death. Fellowship with a faithful group of believers will strengthen our walk with God (1 John 1:7).